FORWARD/COMMENTARY

The National Institute of Standards and Technology (NIST) is a measurement standards laboratory, and a non-regulatory agency of the United States Department of Commerce. Its mission is to promote innovation and industrial competitiveness. Founded in 1901, as the National Bureau of Standards, NIST was formed with the mandate to provide standard weights and measures, and to serve as the national physical laboratory for the United States. With a world-class measurement and testing laboratory encompassing a wide range of areas of computer science, mathematics, statistics, and systems engineering, NIST's cybersecurity program supports its overall mission to promote U.S. innovation and industrial competitiveness by advancing measurement science, standards, and related technology through research and development in ways that enhance economic security and improve our quality of life.

The need for cybersecurity standards and best practices that address interoperability, usability and privacy has been shown to be critical for the nation. NIST's cybersecurity programs seek to enable greater development and application of practical, innovative security technologies and methodologies that enhance the country's ability to address current and future computer and information security challenges.

The cybersecurity publications produced by NIST cover a wide range of cybersecurity concepts that are carefully designed to work together to produce a holistic approach to cybersecurity primarily for government agencies and constitute the best practices used by industry. This holistic strategy to cybersecurity covers the gamut of security subjects from development of secure encryption standards for communication and storage of information while at rest to how best to recover from a cyber-attack.

Why buy a book you can download for free?   We print this so you don't have to.

Some are available only in electronic media. Some online docs are missing pages or barely legible.

We at 4th Watch Publishing are former government employees, so we know how government employees actually use the standards. When a new standard is released, an engineer prints it out, punches holes and puts it in a 3-ring binder. While this is not a big deal for a 5 or 10-page document, many NIST documents are over 100 pages and printing a large document is a time-consuming effort. So, an engineer that's paid $75 an hour is spending hours simply printing out the tools needed to do the job. That's time that could be better spent doing engineering. We publish these documents so engineers can focus on what they were hired to do – engineering. It's much more cost-effective to just order the latest version from Amazon.com

If there is a standard you would like published, let us know. Our web site is Cybah.webplus.net

NIST Advanced Manufacturing Series 300-4

Guide to Industrial Wireless Systems Deployments

Richard Candell
Mohamed Hany
Kang B. Lee
Yongkang Liu
Jeanne Quimby
Kate Remley

This publication is available free of charge from:
https://doi.org/10.6028/NIST.AMS.300-4

National Institute of
Standards and Technology
U.S. Department of Commerce

NIST Advanced Manufacturing Series 300-4

Guide to Industrial Wireless Systems Deployments

Richard Candell
Kang B. Lee
Engineering Laboratory

Mohamed Hany
Yongkang Liu
Information Technology Laboratory

Jeanne Quimby
Kate Remley
Communications Technology Laboratory

This publication is available free of charge from:
https://doi.org/10.6028/NIST.AMS.300-4

April 2018

U.S. Department of Commerce
Wilbur L. Ross, Jr., Secretary

National Institute of Standards and Technology
Walter Copan, NIST Director and Undersecretary of Commerce for Standards and Technology

Acknowledgements

The authors would like to acknowledge the NIST industrial wireless technical working group (IWSTWG) members for their valuable contributions to the content of this document.

Al Salour, Boeing Research & Technology
Arturo Angel, Omron Automation Americas
Cheng-Jen (Allen) Chen, Innovatech Solutions
Justin Shade, Phoenix Contact
Kim Fung Tsang, City University of Hong Kong
Mark Vanhorne, The Boeing Company
Penny Chen, Yokogawa America
Sebti Foufou, University of Burgundy
Sterling Rooke, X8, LLC.
Tatyana Passate, Ford Motor Company
Toshi Hasegawa, Yokogawa Electric Corp.
Victor Huang, IEEE, Standards Chair, Industrial Electronics Society
Zhibo Pang, ABB

Disclaimer

Certain commercial equipment, instruments, materials, or systems are identified in this paper in order to specify the experimental procedure adequately. Such identification is not intended to imply recommendation or endorsement by the National Institute of Standards and Technology, nor is it intended to imply that the materials or equipment identified are necessarily the best available for the purpose.

Table of Contents

List of Tables

List of Figures

1 INTRODUCTION

1.1 Executive Summary

Wireless technology has greatly transformed our world. Influenced by the proliferation of smartphones and tablets, the use of wireless technology in industry has transformed work being performed and continues to grow at a rapid pace. Wireless technology has great appeals to many manufacturers, for example, industrial automation systems, which include process control, discrete manufacturing, and safety systems. Applying wireless technologies in new or existing industrial systems for monitoring and controlling equipment and processes eliminates costly cabling and enables configuration flexibility. In addition, using wireless technologies can improve plant-floor operating conditions, performance, and efficiency in emerging smart manufacturing practices.

Wireless technology has been used in industry for many years, for example, the licensed bands, which have the advantage of interference-free operation in general. It has provided years of reliable communications for monitoring and controlling processes, where using cables is either too costly or impractical. When interference is encountered, there is always legal recourse. In recent years, license-free wireless technologies based on the industrial, scientific, and medical (ISM) radio frequency (RF) bands are proliferating and providing industry many options for solution choices, such as wireless networking for mobile workers and wireless sensor networks for process optimization and asset management. However, the explosive growth of such technologies would cause potential interference problems. In addition, adoption and use of wireless technology has often been hampered by a perceived lack of reliability, integrity, and security, especially when wireless communication is often corrupted or disrupted in harsh industrial settings. So, which wireless technology is best for your application and what approach and precautions should be taken to ensure reliable operation? Simply speaking, there is no one single solution for wireless, since it depends on communication distance between devices, RF requirements, network topology, communication protocol, data rate, network size, and amount of interference in the industrial environment. Thus, understanding the capabilities and applications of wireless technologies will allow users to realize the benefits of wireless, while avoiding the problems of misapplication in challenging industrial environments, in which many potential physical obstructions and sources of interference existed.

Through interactions with industry, National Institute of Standards and Technology (NIST) researchers understood the need of an industrial wireless guideline document, which will help manufacturers, users, and their technology suppliers to design, assess, select, and deploy secure, wireless systems that can perform dependably in their factory settings and conditions. Thus, NIST organized a joint industrial wireless workshop with IEEE on March 13, 2017[1]. The purpose of the workshop was to explore latest and future wireless technologies for establishing best practice guidelines to help manufacturers and users make confident decisions in selecting and applying appropriate wireless technologies for their plants or factories based on their operating requirements and environments. During the discussion, key elements, such as wireless technology categories and selection, spectrum selection and monitoring, radio frequency (RF) concerns, tools, and methods for testing, and acceptance plan for deployment, etc., were intensely discussed and considered to be included in the guidelines document. At the end of the workshop, a consensus was reached for NIST to organize an ad-hoc working group with the aim to conduct monthly working group meetings to develop a best-practice guidelines document to be published by NIST in September 2018. NIST announced this effort in the Federal Register through "the formation of a technical working group (TWG) to develop best practices guidelines in selecting and deploying industrial wireless solutions within industrial environments, such as process control and discrete manufacturing. Guidelines will consider the entire wireless ecosystem within factories with emphasis on wireless networks operating on the factory floor. This includes factory/plant instrumentation, control systems, and back-haul networks. The guidelines will be technology and vendor agnostic and will address the current needs of industry to have independent guidelines based on user requirements and measurement science research. Volunteers from industry joined the TWG. Through the dedicated work of the TWG members, this document "Guide to Industrial Wireless Systems Deployments" is thus created for industry to use. This document is intended to be a practical guide used by engineers and managers facilitating them to go through the process of defining the objectives of their wireless systems and examining the environments where the wireless systems are to be deployed, then helping them in selecting, designing, deploying, and monitoring the wireless systems using existing technology in a factory. Sufficient background materials about wireless technologies are provided, so that the users have a basic understanding of wireless systems being addressed. Thus, the document is aimed to be a succinct, easy-to-use, reference guide, equipped with checklists throughout the lifecycle of wireless technology from concept and design to deployment and monitoring.

1.2 Purpose and Scope

The purpose of the document is to provide best-practice guidelines for an integrated methodology that aims to enable, assess, and assure the real-time performance of secure wireless systems in smart manufacturing systems. These guidelines also aim to enable users, manufacturers, technology providers, and solution providers to design, select, deploy, configure, and assess robust, safe, reliable, and secure integrated wireless systems, with consideration of any co-existence and interference avoidance issues in smart manufacturing systems. This document will only address existing wireless technologies used in industrial environments. Advanced wireless technologies are outside the scope of the document. A revision of the document may be warranted when new and relevant wireless standards and technologies are adopted and used in industry.

1.3 Intended Audience

This document is intended to be used as a practical guide by control engineers, operational technology professionals, information technology professionals, chief executives, security executives, factory floor managers, and wireless system integrators interested in deploying wireless systems in industrial environments.

1.4 Document Organization

The guidelines document is organized as follows:

- An introduction of the document including an executive summary, purpose and scope, intended audience, and the organization of the document are presented in Chapter 1.
- An introduction to industrial wireless including different wireless technologies and networking basics, as well as radio frequency consideration, wireless terminology, spectrum selection and applicability, and various technical challenges for wireless, such as latency and reliability, are addressed in Chapter 2.
- Business cases for wireless with consideration of the purposes for initiating wireless systems is briefly discussed in Chapter 3.
- A total wireless lifecycle from the objective of choosing wireless to factory survey to candidate selection to wireless policy to deployment to network security and spectrum monitoring are extensively discussed in Chapter 4.
- Wireless for safety operations and related standard(s) are discussed in Chapter 5.
- Industrial wireless security is very important and it should be carefully deployed to protect industrial systems from hacking or attacks. So industrial wireless security issues, practical considerations, and guidelines and standards are addressed in Chapter 6.

- Best wireless practice considerations such as antenna placement, obstructions, path redundancy, shadowing, metal canyons, and RF interference problems are discussed in Chapter 7.
- Various checklists to help wireless systems deployment, such as the Sample Defining Objectives Checklist, Sample Factory Survey Checklist, Sample Candidate Selection Process Checklist, Sample Candidate Requirements Matrix, Sample Wireless Design Checklist, and Sample Wireless Systems Deployment Checklist, are provided in Appendix A.

2 INDUSTRIAL WIRELESS FUNDAMENTALS

2.1 Industrial Control Systems

Industrial systems are those systems that employ machinery to accomplish a set of tasks to produce products or provide a service. Industrial control system (ICS) is a general term that encompasses several types of control systems and associated instrumentation used in industrial technology[2]. This includes supervisory control and data acquisition (SCADA) systems, distributed control systems (DCS), human-machine interfaces (HMI), and other smaller control system configurations such as programmable logic controllers (PLC) and microcontrollers often found in the industrial sectors. Industrial systems can be categorized into different types of systems based on the speed of production or the characteristic of materials and flow.

Industrial systems may be categorized as flow-based, batch-based, or job-based systems. A flow-based system, also called a continuous process, include systems such as oil refineries (Figure 1) and water treatment. Job-based systems, also called discrete manufacturing systems, include the manufacture of machines or products in discrete steps. An aircraft assembly line is an example of a discrete system. Batch-system may be considered a hybrid of discrete and continuous processes. Food production is an example of a batch process. Continuous, discrete, and batch manufacturing processes are quite different in their physical properties, construction, and locality. Continuous processes are often referred to as plants while discrete processes are referred to as factories. Herein, we use the terms plant and factory interchangeably.

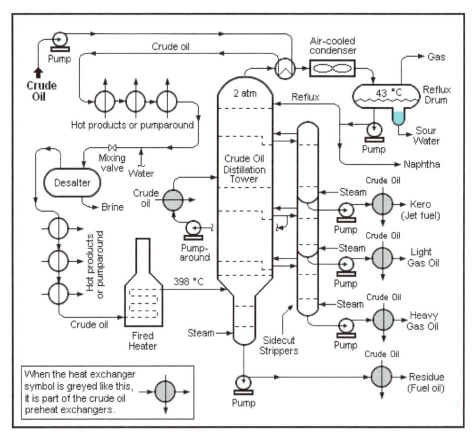

Figure 1. Example of a Continuous Process with liquid or vapor material flow between vessels.

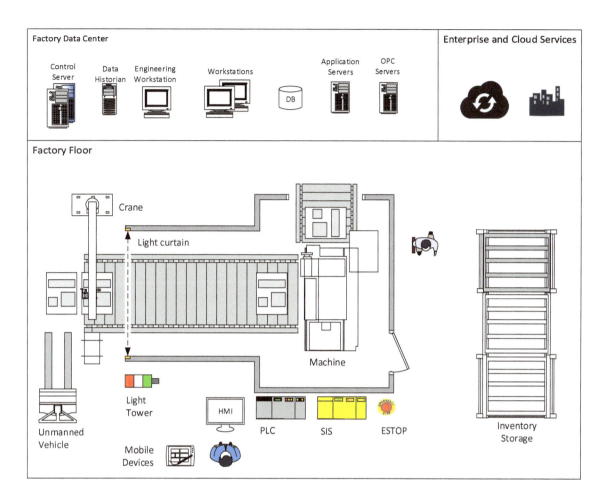

Figure 2. Simplified Discrete Manufacturing Process

Continuous processes include oil refineries as shown in Figure 1, pipelines, chemical plants, water purification, and waste water processes. Materials in continuous processes are typically liquid or gas and undergo heating, cooling, compression, and extraction. Process variables include temperature, pressure, flow, and container level. Actuation typically regards setting of a set-point, speed control of a machine, or controlling flow of material through a valve.

Figure 3. Discrete manufacturing process with robot workers, sensors, and actuators.

Figure 2 illustrates a simplified discrete manufacturing process. Factories will often divide the operation into zones and conduits as described in the industrial automation cyber-security (IACS) standard publication International Electrotechnical Commission (IEC) 62443[3]. Discrete manufacturing operations are divided into the factory floor, a factory data center, the corporate business enterprise, and finally third-party internet or cloud services. The factory floor is then sub-divided into work-cells shown in Figure 3 where specific tasks are performed. In advanced manufacturing operations, work-cells may have reconfigurable purpose for a dynamic task schedule. Within the factory, wireless may be used in place of wires for applications such as input-output (IO) instrumentation, command and control actuation, personnel safety, security and surveillance, asset and vehicle tracking, and back-haul connectivity to the factory data center. By deploying wireless intelligently, factory engineers may better achieve their objectives. Instrumentation within a discrete manufacturing process tends to include ON/OFF sensors such as limit switches, counters, ON/OFF actuators, and communication links carrying command control information for robotic workers. Process information is carried from the work-cells to a centralized data center for additional control decisions and analytics.

2.2 Wireless Technology

Industrial wireless networks (IWNs) are a key enabler of many aspects of advanced manufacturing. IWNs promise lower installation costs compared with wired alternatives, increased operational flexibility, improved factory visibility, and enhanced mobility. Wireless networks are not dissimilar to wired networks with the key exception being the transmission medium. Wired networks typically operate over copper wires, coaxial cable, or fiber optic cable depending on the network type. Wireless networks operate without wires or cables using the electromagnetic propagation. As such, wireless networks operate within a shared medium that is publicly accessible. A listing of wireless technologies is given in Table 1.

Table 1. List of Currently Prevalent Wireless Technologies

Domain	Description
Home and Office	This includes standards-based communications system typically found in the office environment but may be useful for the factory. Includes IEEE 802.11[4] variants and Wi-Fi compliant devices. Bluetooth also falls into this category.
Instrumentation	Includes systems specifically designed for factory operation. IEEE 802.15.4[5] standards such as International Society of Automation (ISA) 100.11a, WirelessHART (IEC 62591:2016), IEC 62601, and ZigBee fall into this category[6]. High-performance standards built on IEEE 802.11 include the Wireless Networks for Industrial Automation - Factory Automation (WIA-FA) IEC 62948[7]. Many exceptional proprietary options exist as well.
Wide Area Sensing	Some applications require the ability to transmit over long distances with minimal power to conserve battery life for sensing and control over wide geographical distances. Examples include LoRaWAN and Sigfox as well as modes of 4G and 5G cellular radio standards.
Other commercial	This category includes systems such as satellite, cellular, directional microwave data links, optical (visible light), and land-mobile radio. This category includes technologies supporting video and voice communication.
Tailored solutions	Includes technologies such as radiating coaxial cable and tropo-scatter solutions that are designed for mission criteria that have unique requirements and require a solution that cannot be met with off-the-shelf alternatives.

2.3 Wireless Networking Basics

2.3.1 Radio Frequency Communication

Radio frequency (RF) communication is used to describe any form of communication that uses electromagnetic spectrum extending from 3 kHz to 300 GHz. Most communications occur between 300 MHz and 6 GHz. The term RF is used synonymously with the term "wireless" although they can have subtle differences in meaning. In RF communication, oscillating electrical current is shaped per the information being transmitted. It is then converted into electric and magnetic fields which propagate together as waves in the surrounding medium which is usually air or vacuum.

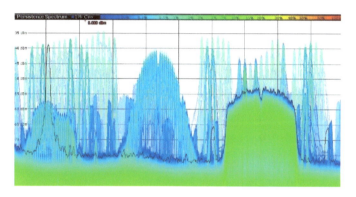

Figure 4. Spectral activity in the 2.4 GHz ISM Band

RF energy will not penetrate easily into conductive materials but will form shallow eddies that reflect most of the energy back into space. Non-conductive materials will usually absorb RF energy thereby causing attenuation. Some materials such as wood and dry-wall will allow RF energy to penetrate through. This effect is common within wood housing and offices which is why home routers work well. Liquids including fog are significant absorbers as are leaves and trees. Absorption properties depend on the frequency of transmission. In general, lower frequency RF waves penetrate walls and lose energy slower than high frequency RF waves. To receive RF energy, an antenna is required to collect the energy and convert that energy into electrical current which can then be processed electronically and converted into usable data.

RF energy can be visualized using standard test equipment such as a spectrum analyzer. A spectrum analyzer displays RF power versus frequency. Shown in Figure 4 is a capture of activity in the 2.4 GHz industrial, scientific, and medical radio (ISM) band. In this capture, Wi-Fi activity exists in the standard channels supporting file transfer, video, and voice communications. Activity from wireless sensor instrumentation also exists producing narrowband frequency hopping transmissions. Since both transmissions co-exist in the same RF band, these devices may interfere with each other. Other devices such as cell phones with active 2.4 GHz hot spots and microwave ovens could also contribute to interference.

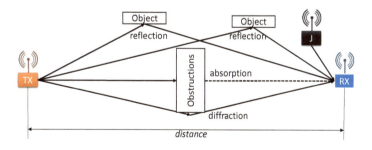

Figure 5. Wireless range, obstructions, absorption, reflection, diffraction, jamming.

Objects within the surrounding environment determine the behavior of the waves as they propagate through the environment. Shown in Figure 5 is a simplified model of a radio channel. When RF energy is transmitted, it will travel in the direction determined by the antenna gain pattern. Objects in the environment may obstruct, attenuate, or reflect RF energy. Reflections contribute to a phenomenon known as multi-path. Edges of objects may also result in diffraction even if a line-of-sight (LOS) path exists. Refer to the explanation of the First Fresnel Zone in Section 7.1. At the receiver end, direct path and reflected energy is detected and decoded into useful information if the signal energy was high enough to overcome naturally and artificially occurring noise and interference. Multi-path reflections may result in significant interference and information loss even if signal power is high.

2.3.2 RF Considerations

The following terms and definitions will help the reader to better understand the vocabulary used in wireless technology and have a stronger understanding of wireless networking considerations.

2.3.2.1 General Concepts and Definitions

Antenna – A device that converts electrical energy into propagating electromagnetic waves or the reverse.

Antenna Polarity – The orientation of the directionality of electromagnetic waves produced by an antenna. Common polarities are vertical, horizontal, and circular. Receive antennas should be oriented such that its polarity matches that of the transmitting antenna polarity.

Bandwidth – The amount of spectrum occupied by a signal. For example, a standard IEEE 802.11g transmission will use a nominal 22 MHz of bandwidth. An IEEE 802.15.4 transmission on which ZigBee, WirelessHART, and ISA100 Wireless are designed will use a nominal 5 MHz of bandwidth.

Carrier – A single frequency sinusoidal signal represented by a vertical line or spike in frequency.

Channel – A term used to identify a physical communications link and includes the characteristics of the entire path of information flow from transmitter to receiver. A channel is defined by electrical and electromagnetic characteristics of the transmission medium such as bandwidth and distortions.

Interference – RF power, typically in the RF band of interest, that disrupts communications by inhibiting the ability of a receiver to decode a transmission. Sources of interference could include anything that radiates electromagnetic (EM) energy such as machinery and undesirable radio devices.

Signal-to-Noise Ratio (SNR) – Ratio of signal power to naturally occurring emissions such as thermal noise and cosmic background radiation. Maximizing SNR is the primary goal of wireless communications.

Signal-to-Noise-And-Interference Ratio (SNIR) – Ratio of signal power to the sum of naturally occurring noise power and interference power. Minimizing the contribution of interference to SNIR is an important goal of a wireless communications system.

Power Decibels – A logarithmic representation of a voltage or power relative to a reference. Power is converted to decibels by the equation $P = 10\log_{10} p$. The notation *dBW* and *dBm* represent power levels relative to 1 Watt and 1 milliwatt, respectively. The notation *dB* denotes a ratio of two numbers and should not be used to denote power.

Link Budget – Calculations that predict the probability that a transmission will be successfully detected and decoded by the receiver. A link budget will account for transmission power, signal formatting, noise, signal distortions, interference, receiver characteristics, and the link reliability requirements.

Link Margin – The difference in decibels (dB) between the ability of a receiver to successfully receive a transmission and the expected minimum received power. A link margin of 10 dB indicates that a signal could be attenuated by an additional factor of 10 before it can no longer be received. A link margin should accommodate reasonable unexpected attenuations, distortions, and interference not directly addressed by the link budget.

2.3.2.2 Transmitter Concepts and Definitions

Transmitter – The device responsibility for transmitting information wirelessly.

Transmit Power – the average amount of RF energy per unit power emitted by the transmit antenna. This is typically specified in Watts, dBW, or dBm.

Bit Rate – The average or peak amount of data transmitted during an interval of time. This is represented as bits per second (bps).

Duty Cycle – The percentage at which a transmitter is active.

Modulation – The method by which information is used to modify the behavior of an RF carrier. Different modulations exist such as amplitude modulation (AM), frequency modulation (FM), and phase modulation (PM). Digital modulations are discrete versions of the above modulations. Common modulations used in industrial communications include binary phase shift keying (BPSK), quadrature phase shift keying (QPSK), and quadrature amplitude modulation (QAM), among others. Wi-Fi uses a combination of BPSK, QPSK, and QAM depending on channel quality.

Error Control Coding (ECC) – A method to increase reliability of a communications link by adding data redundancy that can detect and correct errors produced by the channel. ECC increases the amount of bandwidth requirements or decreasing the amount of useful information over a channel.

Frequency Hopping (FH) – A process by which the carrier frequency is changed during or between transmissions accordingly to a pre-defined synchronized method. With FH, transmitter and receiver must tune to the same frequency at precisely the same time. FH hopping adds a layer of complexity to a system but also makes interception or disruption of the wireless system more difficult, thereby making the system more reliable.

Spread Spectrum – A process of spreading RF energy beyond what is needed to transmit information for the purpose of improved medium access, better interference immunity, or minimization of signal detection.

Payload – The information being transmitted. The size of the payload factors into transmission duration. All communication systems have a limit to the size of a payload before fragmentation is required. Not all communication systems support fragmentation. At the lowest layers of a communication system, the payload includes all data encoding and framing.

2.3.2.3   Receiver Concepts

Receiver – The device responsible for decoding incoming transmissions in accordance with an established protocol.

Received Signal Strength Indicator (RSSI) – A measurement of received signal power.

Received Signal Quality Indicator (RSQI) – A measurement of the quality of the received signal

Sensitivity – The minimum signal strength, SNR, or SNIR required by a receiver to decode an incoming transmission.

Adjacent Channel Interference (ACI) – RF energy that is adjacent to the channel containing a desired signal.

Adjacent Channel Rejection (ACR) – The ability of the receiver to suppress ACI.

Dynamic Range – The difference between the maximum and minimum received signal power. A large dynamic range is particularly helpful in accommodating strong ACI that leaks past RF filtering.

Selectivity – The ability of a device to decode a transmission on one frequency without interference from transmissions on other frequencies.

2.3.2.4 Electromagnetic Interference

Electromagnetic interference (EMI) is always present to some degree in a wireless network. EMI when in the radio frequency spectrum creates a disturbance that disrupts intended communications. The disturbance can degrade performance by introducing RF energy into the circuits of wireless devices. When the disturbance is strong enough to overcome the intended signal, communication loss will result. Sources of EMI include both man-made and natural sources. Natural radio sources typically will not interfere with network operation as the devices or deployment locations are designed to accommodate some natural interference. Man-made interference can include other competing radio devices that operate in the same frequency band or nearby in frequency. Noise from rotating electrical motors can also occur and typically affects radio bands below 400 MHz. Common interference sources include personal devices such as cell-phones in which the Wi-Fi hotspot is enabled. It can also include non-communication devices such as micro-wave ovens. EMI can also emanate from intentional radio jammers designed to disrupt communications.

2.3.2.5 Human Wireless Exposure

Wireless emissions exposure is a recognized concern. The National Institute for Occupational Safety and Health (NIOSH) conducts research on protecting workers from proven and possible EMF health risks due to exposure to radio frequency and other types of emissions. The International Commission on Non-Ionizing Radiation Protection (ICNIRP) of the World Health Organization (WHO) also publishes guidance on radio frequency radiation exposure limits. The Federal Communications Commission (FCC) posted OET BULLETIN 56 [8], "Questions and Answers about Biological Effects and Potential Hazards of Radiofrequency Electromagnetic Fields" which was last updated in 1999. This bulletin, outlines maximum permissible levels of exposure for occupational controlled exposure and uncontrolled exposure.

2.3.3 Networking Considerations

Most networking systems are built upon a layered architecture called the Open Systems Interconnect (OSI) model [9]. Functional layers within the OSI model serve a logical purpose to facilitate a communication service and are shown in Table 2. In a wireless network, layers 1 and 2 of the protocol stack includes all the framing, medium access, error correction coding, modulation, and transmission of a signal. Above those layers are the layers used for logical addressing, connection establishment, and retransmission in case of errors. Layer 2 is responsible for hardware level addressing and framing. The medium access control (MAC) address is used by Layer 2. The network layer, Layer 3, is responsible for logical addressing, routing, and traffic control. For protocols such as Wi-Fi, the Internet Protocol (IP) addresses are used in Layer 3. IP addresses are then associated with MAC addresses.

Table 2. OSI Network Protocol Model

#	Layer	Protocol Data Unit	Purpose
7	Application	Data	High-level interfaces or applications
6	Presentation		Network to application encoding
5	Session		Management of data exchange
4	Transport	Segment/Datagram	Connection and reliability between nodes
3	Network	Packet	Addressing, routing, traffic control
2	Data Link	Frame	Physical addressing and framing
1	Physical	Bit	Transmission and reception of raw signals
Physical Medium (air, space, waveguide, etc.)			

Layers 5 and 6 are not always necessary and may be combined with higher layers. Layer 7, the Application layer, serves as the interface to the functions of the system that use wireless communication service. It includes an application programming interface (API) that allows programs to access the protocol stack. In a wireless sensor, for example, all functional elements would be implemented to connect to a network, transmit sensor readings, receive commands, manage reliability, and maintain connections. A microcontroller or processor within the wireless sensor device would access the wireless network through the Application Layer API.

A network logically consists of nodes and logical connections or edges between the nodes. Depending on the design of the network, nodes can be organized into different topologies. A topology defines how nodes within a network are arranged. Shown in Figure 6 are various network topologies including a peer-to-peer (P2P) single hop, P2P multi-hop, star, and mesh topologies. A single-hop P2P topology is used for directed communications between two nodes. A microwave link between two buildings or a link between a tank farm and central office are examples of a single-hop topology. A multi-hop topology is an extension of single-hop where distance between nodes is a concern and additional range is required.

More complex topologies include the star topology and the mesh topology. Star topologies also known as "hub and spoke" are designed to have a central mediator such as an access point in a home/office wireless network. Through the star topology, nodes can communicate together through the central node. The central node in a star topology coordinates communication within the network. In mesh topologies, nodes within the network can communicate directly with other nodes without the need for a central node. Star topology networks typically have better delay determinism than mesh networks because the hopping is determined before deployment. An example of a star topology industrial wireless network is ISA100.11a. Wi-Fi and other IEEE 802.11 variants are also usually star topology networks by default.

A mesh network will have better reliability because data may be routed through alternate nodes in the network, but it achieves this reliability at the expense of deterministic delay. Mesh networks can be configured to have deterministic latency under normal operating circumstances. Examples of mesh networks are WirelessHART and ZigBee. The ISA100.11a network can be configured to behave as a mesh,

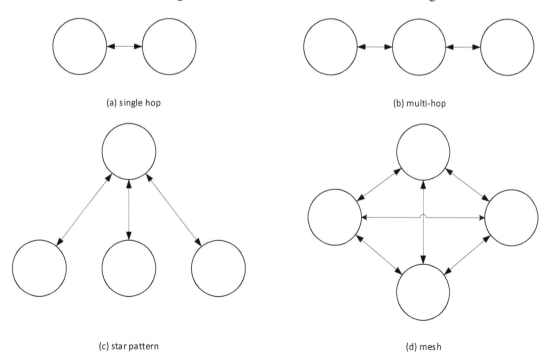

Figure 6. Illustrations of different network topologies.

but it's default is the star topology to ensure reliability and latency determinism. A Wi-Fi network can also be configured as a mesh network.

Other important considerations for the wireless network are now discussed. These considerations have impacts on the selection, deployment, and maintenance of the network and should be considered carefully.

Addressing – How the network identifies nodes. An address is a unique identifier that the network uses to establish connections and route information. The addressing scheme used by a network will limit the number of devices that the wireless system can support.

Naming – A human-readable identifier for a node or device within a network. Addressing the network may support identification that would be useful for a human to identify a device within the network.

Network Throughput – The amount of useful information that can traverse the network within a finite amount of time. Throughput must be measured as useful information; therefore, a specification of throughput should not include network overhead such as packet headers and acknowledgements. Throughput within a wireless network will depend greatly on the conditions of the network and the topology of the network. Single routing points such as what is shown in Figure 7 can become stress points within a network limiting throughput under changing RF conditions and can also be a single point of failure as one node will be the conduit for one section of the network.

Number of Devices – A wireless network will have a limit in the number of devices that it can support. More devices on the network will have an impact on the reporting rates that are possible and may contribute to self-interference depending on the type of network used.

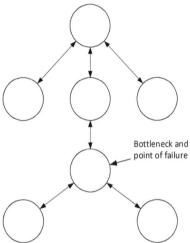

Figure 7. Illustrations of a network bottleneck at a single router node.

Reliability – In a wireless network, reliability is a measure of the probability that a logical data path between a source and destination within a network, such as a sensor and a PLC, is available such that data will be received by its intended recipient within specified time constraints. This should not be confused with metrics associated with low-level packet transmissions within the network such as packet error rate. Reliability within an industrial network is a measure of likelihood that information will be guaranteed to be received by an intended consumer on-time. For example, a proximity sensor reading within a mesh network could be delivered within a 100ms deadline to a PLC for feedback control with 99.999% success. Reliability is one of the most important factors in a automation and control networks

Latency – In general, latency is the time that it takes for data to travel from its source to its destination. For industrial sensing applications, this is more aptly defined as the time delay from when a measurement is taken and delivered to its intended recipient. For industrial actuation and control, it is the time from when a command is issued to when it is received by its intended recipient and action begins. Latency in an industrial system includes the physical measurement and actuation process.

Encryption – A method used to encode data to prevent unauthorized access to the data. Encryption is important to protecting intellectual property information that may be construed by observing data traversing a factory network. While a wireless network utilizes the electromagnetic spectrum, which is an open natural resource, this does not mean that data is not secure. Like wired networks, wireless networks can employ strong encryption which defends against unauthorized data access. It is important then to verify that the level of encryption that a candidate wireless network uses will meet the needs of the security risk level of the factory.

Authentication – A method used to validate that a device or user is authorized to gain network access and that the source of data is genuine. Authentication is an important aspect of factory security linked to process availability and can be more important than encryption. Devices within a network should be authenticated. Wireless networks should support device authentication. Management services supporting the network should support user authentication. User passwords should be updated regularly and default passwords should never be used.

Key management – The set of management tools, protocols, and procedures for updating keys for devices in the field and those already deployed. Some systems require keys to be loaded by physically touching the device whereas other systems can perform this task remotely through a service called over-the-air rekeying (OTAR). When a device is deployed, it may be impractical and costly to locate the device and send personnel to the device to load new keys. A wireless system that supports OTAR capabilities will improve the maintainability of the system.

Over-the-air programming (OTAP) – A capability that allows a device or devices to be reconfigured or reprogrammed once it is deployed. Like OTAR, new configuration parameters for devices such as a change in reporting rate would be made easier with OTAP. Intelligent devices that can be reprogrammed with new software may also use OTAP capabilities to make deployment of the software easier.

Over-the-air-rekeying (OTAR) – A capability in which data signal encryption "code" keys are updated in secure information systems by conveying the keys through encrypted wireless communication channels.

Power Source – The source of electrical power. In some plants and factories, power is easily accessible, and in some access to power is limited. The type of power greatly determines the capabilities of the wireless system and devices. If a wired power source is available, it should be used instead of batteries as batteries require periodic replacement. Batteries are useful as a backup to wired power sources especially for mission-critical applications. Other sources of power include solar power and piezoelectric power from vibrations. Solar power is a good way of powering wireless devices if ample light is available and dust in the environment does not cover the solar cells over time.

Reboot/Reorganization Time – This is the amount of time that it takes to reboot all network devices that have lost power and to re-establish the network. After power is re-established, it takes time for devices to boot and for connections to be made. Some wireless systems will take seconds to reconnect a device to the network. Other systems could take minutes per device which could lead to hours for all devices in a power outage where key devices such as a router or gateway lose power. This concern exemplifies the need for stable and reliable power sources. Under extreme situations, an RF interferer could cause the same type of network condition if the interference is powerful enough and persists for a long time. Each wireless system has strengths and weaknesses in this area, and systems should be carefully evaluated against mission objectives before being deployed.

Intrinsic Safety – A protection technique for safe operation of electrical equipment in hazardous areas by limiting the energy, electrical and thermal, available for ignition. Areas with dangerous concentrations of flammable gases or dust are found in applications such as petrochemical refineries and mines. Wireless devices may be labeled with an intrinsic safety rating. Intrinsic safety is defined by The National Fire Protection Association (NFPA) 70E Standard for Electrical Safety in the Workplace[10].

2.4 Wireless Applicability and Technical Challenges

Wireless has many advantage over wired installations, and it has many challenges. Applications of factory wireless can include process monitoring, condition alarming, product and asset tracking, supervisory control, and feedback control. Use of wireless will depend on expected cost savings over wired options and the technical requirements of the application. Technical requirements can often be linked to the mobility, latency, loss, and scale constraints. Table 3 lists the latency, loss, and scale requirements of typical classes of industrial applications[11]. Note that while this table lists typical constraints, every application is different. Constraints can vary and easily exceed the limits specified in the table. Users must understand the requirements of their respective systems before embarking on any wireless enhancement. Latency here refers to the time difference between when an event is sensed and when it is received by another actor within the system. Loss is a measure of how well events are communicated on time within a system. Packet error rate can be used to describe loss but should not be confused with loss since loss is an end-to-end measure that includes more than the communication system. Scale is a count of the number of nodes on the network. Networks have limitations on the number of supported nodes. It is also important to acknowledge that more nodes can mean slower reporting rates which impact latency.

Table 3. List of Typical Network Reliability and Latency Requirements for Industrial Systems

Application Class	Latency, l	Pr. Loss, r	Devices, S
Monitoring	$l < 1\,\mathrm{s}$	$r < 10^{-5}$	$s < 10\,000$
Supervisory Control			
Flow-based	$l < 100\,\mathrm{ms}$	$r < 10^{-6}$	$s < 30$
Job-based	$l < 100\,\mathrm{ms}$	$r < 10^{-7}$	$s < 10$
Feedback Control			
Flow-based	$l < 10\,\mathrm{s}$	$r < 10^{-6}$	$s < 1000$
Job-based	$l < 10\,\mathrm{ms}$	$r < 10^{-7}$	$s < 10$
Safety Alarming	$l < 1s$	$r < 10^{-7}$	$s < 10$

Since the electromagnetic spectrum otherwise known as the radio frequency (RF) spectrum is a publicly accessible yet a limited natural resource, special consideration must be placed on the selection of the RF operating band for any wireless deployment. These considerations include spectrum availability, bandwidth, impacts on distance and propagation, sources of interference, and security concerns. A table of wireless applicability is given in Table 8 in Appendix B. The reader is encouraged to consult this table for guidance when selecting a technology for their application.

2.5 Electromagnetic Spectrum Governance

The electromagnetic spectrum (EM) is a limited natural resource. Of the possible frequency bands available for use, only a fraction of spectrum is available for legal commercial use. Within the United States, the electromagnetic spectrum is regulated by the Federal Communications Commission (FCC) and the National Telecommunications and Information Administration (NTIA). The FCC has authority over non-federal communications while the NTIA is concerned with federal communications. Use of the electromagnetic spectrum will require authorization in some form from either of the two agencies. Radio frequency allocations [12] for the United States is shown in Figure 8. For most industrial establishments, FCC authorization is

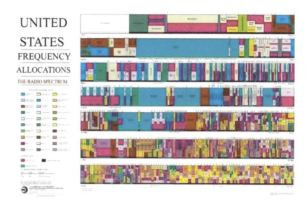

Figure 8. United States radio spectrum frequency allocations chart.

included in the system being procured. For federal industrial establishments, NTIA authorization is required to operate in a licensed band.

2.5.1 Licensing

Use of the EM spectrum is divided into two categories, licensed and unlicensed spectrum. Licensed spectrum requires FCC authorization for each specific use or device. Unlicensed spectrum such as the industrial, scientific, and medical radio (ISM) band is deemed a public resource and includes the 902 to 928 MHz, 2.400 to 2.4835 GHz, and 5.725 to 5.875 GHz radio bands. Industrial wireless devices typically operate over these unlicensed bands. While many wireless systems are designed to operate over the ISM bands, the systems will be subjected to the interference from other devices using the bands. Licensed spectrum has fewer wireless systems options, but it provides a better guarantee of available spectrum to operate devices without interference from others wireless systems.

Coordination with bordering nations is required for licensed RF applications in proximity to those borders. Furthermore, all devices operating within the United States including those purchased from a foreign source must have an FCC identifier. An FCC ID is a unique identifier assigned to a device registered with the United States Federal Communications Commission. For legal sale of wireless devices in the United States, wireless device manufacturers must have the device evaluated by an independent laboratory to ensure it conforms to FCC standards.

2.5.2 RF Spectrum Planning and Internal Governance

Use of licensed and unlicensed RF bands are regulated by the FCC; however, it is advisable that organizations track and manage their use of the RF spectrum beyond what is required by the FCC. Tracking of wireless devices and networks in terms of their spectral usage will help the organization plan for deployments, manage growth, identify interference sources, and avoid network conflicts. Use of licensed bands may help to avoid interference, but all RF bands have limited capacity resources, and, hence, planning is important for its effective use. Having a method for internal governance within a factory enterprise is an essential part of a factory spectrum planning and monitoring strategy. Internal governance should be implemented as a governing board with managers and engineers that agree on the short-term and long-term strategies for use of the EM spectrum within the proximity and confines of their operations. The internal governance should account for the long-term vision of wireless deployments within the factory.

3 BUSINESS CASE FOR WIRELESS

One of the key enablers of factory automation is the availability of wireless radio frequency devices. Some applications of radio frequency devices include process control, oil and gas refineries, pharmaceuticals, food and beverage, autonomous guided vehicles (AGVs) control, slotted microwave guides, pendants to control cranes and machine tools, active and passive radio frequency identifier (RFID) for tracking parts, tools and consumables, wireless barcode readers, remote sensing of critical process parameters, mobile telephony, door openers, emergency communication, and general factory Wi-Fi for internet connectivity. In addition, devices not directly associated with the manufacturing process such as microwave ovens and mobile telephone hot spots must be included when designing a factory wireless system. As useful as wireless communications is, it must be recognized that spectrum is limited and there must be judicious choices about when it should be used, and when wired connections are preferable.

In general terms, wireless (as with any upgrade to a factory or enterprise system) should satisfy a requirement related to quality, reliability, efficiency, safety, regulation, or environment as shown in Table 4. The requirements pertain to the business enterprise which in the case of a manufacturing operation means the plant or factory. A wireless deployment should be designed to satisfy one of the key business concerns listed.

Table 4. Purposes for initiating a wireless systems deployment

Functionality	Is wireless required to achieve an aspect of function within the factory operation? For example, does the factory require a mobility to achieve a goal?
Reliability	Is reliability of the production line improved? The ability to manufacture products, parts or assemblies which conform to the engineering definition, and can demonstrate conformity.
Safety	Are people or equipment made safer? The ability of employees to perform their jobs free from recognized hazards including falls, hazardous energy, confined space, ergonomics, and hazardous materials, and being able to demonstrate compliance with all safety regulations.
Efficiency	The ability to meet target costs and continue forever to reduce unit production costs.
Quality	The ability to manufacture parts and assemblies which conform to the engineering definition, and be able to demonstrate conformity.
Environment	Will the environment be better protected or accidents be avoided?
Regulation	The ability to demonstrate compliance with applicable government regulations at the city, county, state, and federal level.

4 WIRELESS LIFECYCLE

Selecting an industrial wireless network (IWN) for factory deployment requires careful attention to planning and design as well as deployment strategies and monitoring. And IWN must meet the needs for the functional operation of the plant or factory and satisfy the long term operational goals of the organization.

Shown in Figure 9 is the generalized lifecycle of a wireless system deployment. Once a need for a networking solution is identified and wireless is deemed a worthwhile solution to consider, several steps should be undertaken from the time that the need is identified to the time in which a wireless system is deployed. The following sections defined the process guidelines for a wireless systems deployment. It should not be construed as a formal change management process that would replace an existing and well-established process within an organization. Change and configuration management are important considerations for all organizations, and many resources exist to support that process; however, the topic of change and configuration management is not within the scope of this document. These process guidelines should be used to inform or enhance mature processes or help to establish a new process within an organization. The process shown in Figure 9 should also be construed to include feedback between phases. For example, if during the candidate selection phase, it is determined that key performance indicators were omitted, then it would be necessary to refine the objectives to accommodate necessary changes.

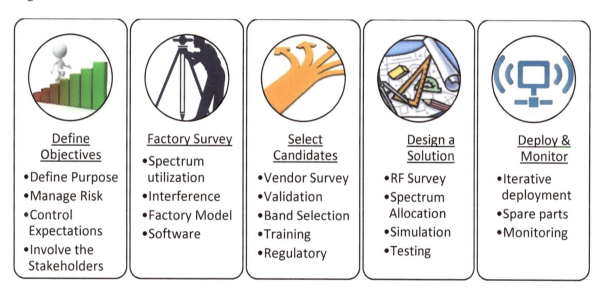

Figure 9. Lifecycle Components of Wireless Systems Deployment

When embarking on a wireless enhancement, and the organization deploying such a network is inexperienced with wireless deployments, it may be prudent to begin with a small deployment or proof-of-concept. This will allow the organization to learn about wireless while developing a process for wireless deployments. If an immediate massive deployment is necessary for an inexperienced organization, a system integrator who is experienced with large-scale wireless deployments will become vital to the success of the system. An experienced system integrator should be expected to cooperate with factory engineers who wish to implement the guidance provided within this document. A system integrator cannot replace the due diligence of the factory engineers to oversee the project and select appropriate technologies for their operation.

The first step in the process is the Identification of Need. Each entity will have a vision for why a factory enhancement is necessary. It is here that the objectives and success criteria will be defined and that a wireless system may be considered. The next step is the site survey in which the factory environment is analyzed comprehensively to determine the requirements for candidate solutions. Once the survey has taken place and data is readily available from the survey, candidate systems will be selected. Following candidate selection, a solution will be developed and tested. Performance will be validated against the original requirements, and a deployment plan will be devised. The end result is a deployed solution or iteration that meets the technical requirements and effectively addresses the original business goals. It is important to understand the steps of conducting the site survey, identifying candidates, designing a solution, and deployment may be an iterative process. Iterative design is a proven and effective means to manage risk.

4.1   Define Objectives

Before embarking on a wireless systems program within a factory, the business requirements, i.e., the purpose of the factory enhancement, should be fully understood, documented, and shared among the stakeholders within the organization. Defining objectives clearly and concisely enables support from within the organization and a successful deployment.

Defining the objectives will include identifying the reason for beginning a factory enhancement. The organization should first ask the question: What is the benefit of the factory improvement to the organization? Section 3 provides a list of success criteria that may be used to drive the implementation of a wireless system or any factory enhancement program. These criteria include reliability improvements, improvements in safety for humans and machinery, a reduction in operating cost, product quality improvements, environmental stewardship, and regulatory compliance. Objectives must be communicated to management and stakeholders. Realistic technological expectations are defined for the wireless deployment and communicated to stakeholders. Performance will be ascertained based on measurement data not supposition.

Wireless technology will not serve all applications. For example, a safety integrated system demands reliable communications between the safety controller and its sensors and actuators. Wireless is low risk for applications such as to enable Industrial Internet of Things (IIoT) deployments, factory monitoring, supervisory control, and backup systems to wired. Wireless for safety should address quality of service requirements for the use case. Wireless systems do not directly address the reliability and latency requirements of feedback control applications with real-time constraints, but depending on the physical system requirements, it is possible. Even with developments in wireless technology, a technical solution is not always possible with respect to addressing security threats such as jamming and other forms of interference. In such a case, optical wavelength communication may be better suited for such applications. Therefore, when using wireless for feedback control and safety, a careful risk analysis is required. When using wireless for safety monitoring, the ISA 84 WG8 technical report may be used as a deployment guide [13]. A general reference for wireless applicability is given in Table 5. Since technologies can differ and improve over time, this table should be used as a rule-of-thumb.

Success of the wireless deployment depends on the purpose of the system and measurable objectives. Wireless may be one component of the overall factory enhancement. Referring to Table 4, the purpose of the wireless deployment may be to improve reliability, reduce costs, or comply with a new regulation. It is important that those goals be measurable. Measurement methods and metrics should be selected and agreed upon by the stakeholders. Objectives should be documented and managed using the organization's established procedures.

As an example, a cost reduction program may be approached with an IIoT data collection system. After sufficient data is collected, an optimization algorithm could be used to identify points of process improvement such as process tuning, robot insertion, and work scheduling. Achievable cost saving targets would then be agreed upon and the upgrade would commence. In this simple scenario, expected data reliability and latency targets of the optimization algorithm should be ascertained prior to moving to the selection of candidates, as those targets would impact selection criteria and performance assessment. If exact figures are not available, simulation could be used to ascertain down-stream performance. An educated evaluation using as much data available during the objectives definition phase will help to set reasonable, measurable objectives while reducing associate risk of failure.

Table 5. General Appropriateness for Industrial Wireless Applications

Application	General Recommendation
Factory and Building Monitoring, IIoT	Yes
Condition Alarming	Yes
Supervisory Control	Yes
Feedback Control Backup to Wired	Yes
Feedback Control Primary	Possible
Safety Monitoring and Alarming	Possible
Personnel Safety	Possible
Safety Integrated Systems (SIS)	Possible[1]

A checklist for Defining Objectives is included in Appendix A-1. These tasks are important to achieving the objectives of the wireless deployment. Clearly enumerated objectives for the factory enhancement are necessary to explain how the wireless network will serve to achieve those objectives.

Once objectives are defined and the role that wireless will take to support those objectives is defined, measurement methodologies will need to be determined. At this point, it is not necessary to exactly define how measurements will take place; however, it is possible to acknowledge that a measurement-based performance assessment is needed and to begin thinking about how to accomplish the measuring.

The enterprise may have plans for future growth beyond the current enhancement. More wireless networks may be needed to achieve future growth requirements of the enterprise. An iterative plan for growth is commonly used to manage technical risk in some organizations, and future factory network enhancements may be envisioned. For example, channels in the 5 GHz ISM band are particularly valuable as they support channel bonding for high throughput applications; therefore, these channels require careful management. It will be helpful to document those plans and establish a vision for the factory network that includes wireless technology such that stages such as candidate selection account for that vision.

A security risk assessment is also necessary at the early stages of the program. A plan to implement security will be an ongoing task for the factory if it hasn't already been established. Many resources exist that will explain how to implement a security program. These resources are discussed in Section 6. A security

---

[1] In general, wireless is not recommended as the primary mode of communication for an SIS, but it could be used as a backup to wired communication. It is recognized that some SIS designs could require wireless as the only practical mode of communication in rare cases.

management plan will be an important part of implementing a security program within the factory enterprise and establishing a secure wireless network.

Wireless networks require bandwidth of the electromagnetic spectrum. Wireless may or may not already be in use within the factory enterprise; therefore, it will be necessary to conduct a preliminary spectral occupancy survey of all wireless networks within the factory as well as all sources of interference to include microwave ovens, employee-owned devices, and outside interference. It will be important to establish the importance of a spectrum management plan if one is not already established. A spectrum management plan will contain an inventory of all known wireless networks and sources of electromagnetic emissions. It will also establish policies and procedures for monitoring the electromagnetic spectrum and taking actions when events occur. Like the security management plan, the spectrum management plan will be an ongoing activity that is essential to running a secure and stable wireless network.

4.2 Factory Survey

A factory survey is a critical part of a successful wireless deployment. With a detailed understanding of the physical environment, RF propagation characteristics, and a full systems inventory will provide valuable data to make the wireless deployment successful. A factory survey includes an assessment of the available RF spectrum, and identification of sources of interference, human safety requirements, and an inventory of factory models, components, interfaces, and requirements. An early RF characterization of the factory environment may be helpful at this stage, but deferring the RF characterization study to the design stage after a candidate solution is selected may be more practical and yield more useful information.

A factory survey checklist is provided in Appendix A-2. The list provides useful considerations in conducting a comprehensive survey of the factory environment. Tailoring of the checklist is encouraged and will depend on enterprise objectives and processes. Considerations covered in the checklist are described in the following sections.

4.2.1 Applicable Physical Inventory

Take a comprehensive inventory of the factory components that are envisioned to come into direct or indirect contact with the wireless network. Factory components could include the following:

physical factory layout – drawings and 2D/3D computer-aid design (CAD) models that depict the physical environment;

measurement and control points – all process variables within the factory/plant process that may be of interest to be monitored or controlled;

machines – all machinery to be included in a prognostic, health monitoring, and control program;

mobile robotic platforms – any machine that can be considered autonomous and controlled remotely;

materials – a list of all parts, products, and raw materials that must be tracked throughout the process;

maintenance tools – a list of all maintenance tools such as power tools that must be tracked;

supervisory and feedback control points – a list of all real-time processors used to supervise and control the operation;

data collection systems – a list of all systems such as databases including interface specifications for each;

data transfer points – a list of all systems that require a broadband data connection for general data or file transfer;

human-machine interfaces – a list of all human machine interface stations and mobile platform, connectivity requirements, and interface specifications;

employee-owned mobile devices – all device types such as tablets and cell-phones that employees will be allowed to have in accordance with factory policies; and

Power sources – a list of all cables and power sources that could be used to supply power to devices.

Table 6. Process Variable Specifications

Inventory	Description
Process variable	The name and purpose of the variable to be monitored or controlled.
Type of process variable	The class of variable, *e.g.,* temperature sensor, pressure sensor, proximity sensor, valve positioner, robot status, etc.
Change rate	This is an assessment of how the variable changes. For continuous processes, this could be the average and maximum rate of change. For discrete processes, this could be the average and maximum rate of state change. Change rate will influence the frequency of reporting.
Amount of data	This is a size or size distribution of the instrumentation payloads or files that will be transmitted.
Delay Tolerance	An assessment of how much can this data be delayed before impacting the operation.
Reliability Tolerance	An assessment of how data loss of this process variable will impact success of the factory enhancement.
Criticality to operation	An assessment of how loss or delay of this process variable will impact the success of the factory enhancement.

4.2.2   Operational Models

Collect any abstract models such as equations, statistics, pseudo code, process flow diagrams, software, and data that are available to simulate the factory or otherwise predict factory behavior. Depending on risk of deploying wireless, running simulations can be a useful tool in predicting data produced by the factory and identifying sensitivity to network resilience issues. Operational models can be used to validate assumptions and assure a better set of technical requirements to be levied on the wireless network.

4.2.3 Identify Process Variable Specifications

Table 6 lists several data points that may be helpful in constructing an effective wireless deployment. Selecting a wireless network specifically for either sensing or control instrumentation will require identifying candidates that can support the specification of signal information or data being communicated.

4.2.4 Identify Safety Issues

Wireless devices could have impacts on the safety within the environment they are used. Some factory environments must meet Intrinsic Safety considerations to prevent fires or explosions. List all safety requirements that will affect the selection criteria of wireless devices.

4.3 Candidate Selection

In the previous two sections, the wireless system requirements were defined and the site of intended operation was surveyed. Using the obtained information, the candidate selection process is initiated where various candidates are identified and their capabilities to satisfy various requirements are evaluated. At this step of the selection process, two stages should be envisioned: 1) Technical Considerations and 2) Candidates evaluation. The first stage includes mapping factory requirements to network candidate capabilities. The second stage includes obtaining information about various candidates, evaluation and validation of the options with information against network requirements, ranking the suitability of candidates, and finally choosing a candidate.

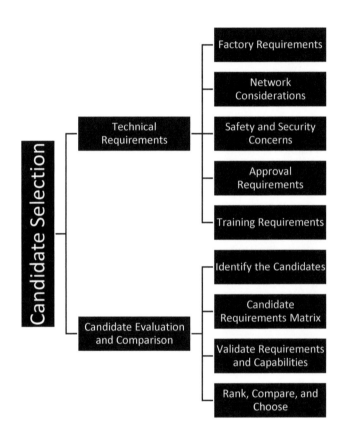

4.3.1 Technical Requirements

The list of factory constraints, network considerations, hard requirements, soft requirements, and applicable regulatory specifications will lead to the evaluation of needed functionality and selection of candidate devices. As candidate capabilities often drive requirements, identification of technical requirements can be done in parallel with candidate identification; however, special caution should be taken to avoid candidates that excessively influence the requirements gathering process. Shown in Appendix A-3 is a candidate selection checklist. Initially, technical requirements should be enumerated and a prioritization or weighting factor will need to be determined as not all requirements are equal in importance. Categories of technical requirements are discussed in the following sections. They include the factory constraints, network requirements, safety, security, regulatory compliance and internal approvals, and training.

4.3.1.1 Factory Requirements and Constraints

Factory requirements were discussed in Section 4.1 where enterprise objectives of deploying wireless networking are defined clearly. The applications where wireless networking benefits are defined include reliability, safety, efficiency, quality, environment and regulatory concerns. Moreover, the criteria for measuring wireless networking performance and its ability to achieve the factory requirements should be clearly defined. Where wireless is used for deterministic applications or other latency and reliability sensitive applications, precise requirements for those applications to include reliability, latency, and scale should be developed. Moreover, factory security considerations will influence the type of wireless networks that will be considered and should be included in the list of technical considerations.

4.3.1.2 Network Considerations

The following concepts are presented as a guide in enumerating the technical requirements.

Functionality and Applications – Based on various required applications, the need of multiple wireless networks is considered due to basic differences in the requirements. As an example, the latency and reliability needs for control loops in discrete manufacturing may require a dedicated wireless network for this type of applications where slow process monitoring has less reliability requirements and hence a different type of wireless networks to be used.

RF Band – While comparing various candidate solutions, the operating RF band will be selected according to performance, factory survey results, spectrum availability, regulatory concerns, and internal governance. It is unreasonable to expect that an RF band will ever be "pristine" without any sources of interference, and the selection of candidates should account for this fact. Requirements may need to account for noise and interference immunity and other practical considerations.

Multi-speed Support – Like the previous point, different applications may work on the same wireless network but with different speeds or response times. As an example, a wireless network may work for all monitoring applications because of the same requirement on the network. The monitored processes may have different rates of change that require different rates of monitoring data transmissions. In this case, the multi-speed support in the candidate wireless network is needed.

Scalability – One of the factory requirements that may validate the need for deploying a wireless network is the future growth of the factory or factory network and the need for more communications devices throughout. This requirement is mapped into the scalability of the candidate networks. For each candidate, the scalability aspects must be discussed including the capacity of the network, ease of network expansion, and the ability to satisfy future growth.

Power Management – The power management requirements are obtained using factory knowledge resulting from the factory site survey. A simple and important example is identification of power sources, types, and locations across the factory. Battery-operated devices use low power for transmission and should have a predictable maintenance schedule for battery replacement. For continuously powered nodes, cabling requirements and structure should be studied and the existing power sources must be defined. Moreover, the power-efficiency of the wireless network should be considered depending on data delivery cost. To quantify power-efficiency, a power analysis of each candidate should be performed to include the number of components, required performance levels, power management schemes, and battery life.

Reliability – Another topic to be considered based on the factory requirements of various applications is the required reliability of the wireless network. That includes the plan of the network to transfer data in situations when the wireless channels are poor. Also, the acceptable off-time of the wireless network has to be defined. Reliability can be measured by the response of the wireless network to various effects. These effects include the RF spectrum usage, the RF agility, the interference immunity, and system power variations such as output power and receiver sensitivity. Moreover, reliability includes various requirements on data delivery including acceptable latency and errors.

Simplicity – Simplicity can be considered in two perspectives. First, the simplicity of the wireless network setup includes the ease of the design, development, and implementation of the wireless network. In this perspective, the candidate wireless networks are considered from the viewpoint of components, tools, and technologies. Programmable components are preferred to allow for more flexibility in designing, implementing, and tuning the wireless network. Second, the simplicity of the wireless network used includes the ease of device activation, network support, monitoring, and tuning of the wireless network.

Range – The expected maximum distance between nodes in the wireless networks should be defined. Range is based on the link budget between any two nodes on a wireless network. Extending the effective range of a network can be accomplished by adjusting power, using a directional antenna, or adding additional nodes to a network to compensate and then deploying routing capabilities which may increase complexity, cost, and power consumption.

Maintainability – During the lifetime of a wireless network, nodes will need both emergency and regular maintenance. The ease of performing these tasks determines the level of maintainability of a candidate wireless solution. It includes both hardware and software maintenance to include part replacement, software upgrades, and reconfigurations. In the case of software maintainability, the user interface and the network management software should be user-friendly.

Interoperability – Due to different applications and functionality, various communications protocols can operate simultaneously; however, those protocols may be incompatible. For factory networks to interoperate, their communications protocols must be compatible and easy to use or adapt. In a wireless sensor network, sensors may report their process information which is transmitted to a gateway. That information is not usable until it can be retrieved by another application such as a PLC program or optimization application. For that to happen, the gateway needs to communicate the information in language (i.e., a protocol) that can be understood. For an example, automation applications have traditionally used Modbus for localized communications between nodes such as a sensing unit and PLC. This allows users to extract the data. Modbus, while easy to implement and quite ubiquitous, lacks language and context that other modern protocols provide.

4.3.1.3 Safety and Security

Although safety and security are part of the factory and network considerations, they have been discussed in a separate subsection due to their importance in protecting data, personnel, and factory assets. Safety and security are discussed in more details in Sections 5 and 6, respectively.

Generally, the levels of required security against malicious attacks for different applications are diverse. Hence, for each candidate wireless network, the level of achieved security and types of security systems must be considered. Also, if using multiple wireless networks, the approach of security in these networks must be considered and whether to use multiple systems that will be managed separately. Security can be divided into three basic categories which are integrity, confidentiality, and availability.

The use of wireless networks in safety applications is primarily motivated by cost, mobility, and ruggedness considerations that wired solutions cannot accommodate. Wireless connections cannot be physically damaged although it can be argued that interference is a form of physical interruption. On the other hand, safety applications requirements can be very strict regarding latency, reliability, and robustness. As a result, while considering candidate systems for safety applications, requirements for these systems should be strictly enforced. The deployed network must always comply with regulatory concerns.

4.3.1.4 Approval Requirements

Determine if the candidates need specific regulatory or external approvals for operation. This includes approvals from entities such as the FCC or other internal governance structure such as a spectrum management group. Also, safety approvals should be considered, such as intrinsic safety ratings, for every wireless node. Hence, a set of acceptable nodes can only be used at certain locations. All internal and external regulatory approvals should be enumerated.

4.3.1.5 Training Requirements

Each candidate will have unique training needs. These training requirements should be identified based on the experience of personnel using the technology. Moreover, the training details should be determined such as how training will be conducted and how knowledge will be disseminated throughout the organization. These training requirements should be defined to handle all installation, operation, and maintenance activities.

4.3.2 Candidate Evaluation and Comparison

Once the requirements and available options are identified, the evaluation and comparison of the possible candidates will help to select the appropriate solution. By enumerating the technical requirements comprehensively, each candidate can be assessed impartially according to the requirements and assigned weights. If it is helpful to do so, a scoring system that summates the weights of compliant requirements can be adopted by the assessment team in selecting candidate solutions. In addition, where requirements are validated through testing, additional weight for those requirements can be applied. This approach gives advantage to solutions that have been independently tested.

4.3.2.1 Identify the Candidates

After establishing all the network requirements, the following step is to identify the potential candidates. As mentioned previously, candidate identification can occur in parallel to the requirements gathering process. The candidates are found through normal channels of internet searches, vendor consultation, discussions with systems integrators, and datasheets. Industrial communications experts and consultants are good sources for identifying candidates as their experience and knowledge of application scenarios and deployment tuning can be helpful. Forums, conferences, and industry shows are good ways of identifying candidates and capabilities.

4.3.2.2 Candidate Requirements Matrix

A candidate requirements matrix (CRM) such as the example given in Appendix A-4 is generated. The CRM contains a list of requirements, weights and priorities, and a list of the identified candidates. By enumerating the quantitative and qualitative requirements, it is then possible to capture requirements compliance. List all the requirements atomically. A measurable specification for each atomic requirement should be recorded in the table. A weighting factor is assigned for each requirement with a value between 0 and 1. A value of 1 indicates the most important or highest priority; whereas, a value less than 1 assigns a lower level of importance. A requirement should not have a value of 0, as that indicates that it is not a requirement.

4.3.2.3 Validate Requirements and Capabilities

At this point, all candidates are assessed for each requirement independently. Some requirements can be satisfied through analysis of datasheets or performance reports from similar systems. Other requirements will require verification by testing within the operating environment of the factory. Validation of a requirement by analysis or by testing will be determined by the selection team. It is important in this validation process to test various system capabilities included in Section 4.3.1.2 such as the integration with existing industrial hardware and running applications, and the performance of the system with the existing level of traffic over the RF spectrum and while the plant is in operation. It is also important to allow the wireless system to run for a period of time based on the applications to make sure it works seamlessly. Tools such as simulation and hardware-in-the-loop (HIL) testbeds are valuable resources to leverage for assessing highly important or high-risk requirements. The results of each validation should be captured in the CRM according to some pre-defined rubric such as the weight scoring system discussed previously.

4.3.2.4 Rank, Compare, and Choose

At this point, a completed CRM has been generated. Those candidates that do not meet the absolute requirements are eliminated. Those candidates that remain will then be compared quantitatively by recording the scores for each candidate. The candidate with the highest score will be selected. This process is illustrated with the candidate scoring matrix in Appendix A-4.

4.4 Solution Design

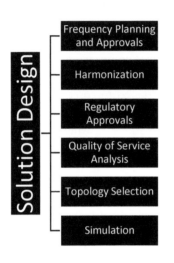

At this stage of building the industrial wireless solution, the best candidate has been selected and it is the time to specify the network architecture, wireless system parameters, and wireless node locations, and validate the capabilities of the solution design. The steps of obtaining the systems design can be listed as planning, analysis, design, simulation, and optimization.

The planning phase includes the frequency planning and the corresponding regulatory and internal approvals. Frequency planning includes channel selection and management. An RF Quality of Service (QoS) analysis can be done by evaluating receive signal power and propagation characteristics given hypothetical transmitter and receiver locations. Results of a QoS study are helpful in selecting locations for network infrastructure and conducting simulations when necessary. The network design phase includes the wireless network architecture, topology selection, and node placement. Many network design aspects can be defined before measurement and analysis but may need to be updated after an analysis of the QoS measurements are available.

Simulation is a good tool for reducing risk associated with complex designs or scenarios involving wireless supervisory or feedback control. Simulation can be useful in predicting performance of a wireless system before a major deployment investment is made. Based on simulation results, final tuning of the design parameters can be performed before deployment.

4.4.1 Frequency Planning and Approvals

During the candidate selection, the operating frequency band of the wireless solution is determined. First, approvals for the use of a certain frequency band need to be obtained as explained in the following subsection. Then, frequency planning should be performed including the study of channel utilization and interference effects, and identification of coverage cells and access points.

During channel utilization, the initiated traffic from each physical point is evaluated based on the physical process requirements. The bandwidth requirement for each connection is determined based on traffic over this connection. It is advisable, if testing can be performed, to verify these calculations. The coverage level and networking connectivity at a certain work space is determined based on total amount transferred data. Depending on the technology used, the number of channels required to cover the work space is determined following the general concept of frequency reuse in various coverage regions.

Using the spectrum survey to identify interference levels, the received signal quality can be estimated to evaluate the requirements for achieving the calculated rate. Finally, the access points requirements are defined to carry traffic between nodes in a coverage region and to carry traffic to other network locations. Furthermore, various applications are considered during this phase including instrumentation, voice, video, backhaul, and safety applications. In most of the cases, different technologies will be deployed for different applications. However, the frequency planning should be done over all the wireless systems.

4.4.2   Regulatory Approvals

Some radio bands require FCC licensing approval before use. Licensed frequencies should be strongly considered in applications where safety is an issue such as lifting with overhead cranes where exclusive use of frequencies

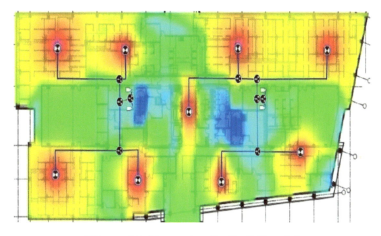

Figure 10. Example of a QoS Heat Map

minimizes the probability of interference and hence a safer operation is achieved. When FCC licensing is required, start the application process early to ensure timely approval, or to provide time to develop alternative solutions if the license application is declined. For frequencies that are not licensed by the FCC, it may be necessary for a manufacturing company to seek approval from an internal governance board to ensure harmonious operations on those frequencies.

4.4.3   Quality of Service Analysis

Conducting a site survey will provide information about how RF transmissions will propagate through the factory given hypothetical transmission points. RF transmissions propagate through the air and will lose power with distance in accordance with a rate of loss. This rate of power loss is influenced by the amount and type of materials present in the environment and the RF band of interest. Radio waves behave differently at 900 MHz than they do at 2.4 GHz or 60 GHz.

Some materials such as steel will reflect RF transmissions creating reflections and a reverberation effect, while other materials such as concrete absorb RF. Reverberation will spread the RF energy over time. While total power is less diminished in a reverberant environment, the time spreading can cause significant distortions and result in data loss and delay. In some cases, reflections can be used to the advantage of the network if distortion is not severe. Most indoor factories fall into the absorptive category. In an absorptive environment, RF transmissions are significantly diminished, but distortion due to time spreading is measurably less.

By identifying potential access points, a coverage map, also called a "heat map," as shown in Figure 10 may be produced that gives an indication of expected quality of service (QoS). A coverage map will provide a graphical perspective about how RF energy permeates the factory environment if locations of wireless infrastructure are known. An RF coverage map can be costly but helpful when attempting to predict through simulation or link budgeting the quality of service for a candidate wireless technology. Each wireless technology has different capabilities. Differences in type and grade of the device matters. A high-end and more expensive wireless device may have a distance that is an order of magnitude better than a less capable device; however, the performance difference may be reflected in the price. Therefore, a heat map provides some perspective of performance, but it should not be used as the single indicator. Overly uniform heat maps may be an indication of faulty measurements or that the simulation was too simplistic. Moreover, the physical factory environment can be very dynamic and the RF characteristic will reflect those changes. Prior to conducting an RF site survey which implies selection of a candidate has been conducted, it is suggested to validate performance of a network during candidate selection using the physical equipment rather than try to predict performance.

Alternatively, NIST performed a high-fidelity propagation analysis of three indoor factory facilities. During this study, NIST measured power loss and delay spread of RF transmissions in three factories. The results of the study were published in NIST Technical Note TN-1951[14]. By using technical information provided in this study, it is possible to predict wireless network performance given transmit power, the sensitivity of the receiving devices, and the nature of the communication channel, i.e., whether the channel is considered line-of-sight (LOS) or non-line-of-sight (NLOS). Strong RF signals are not a definitive indicator of high quality of service within a harsh industrial environment where multi-path reflections dominate. Certainly, signal-to-noise ratio is an important factor, but reflections off factory walls and equipment and the category of the wireless channel (i.e., LOS and NLOS) can dominate performance of the wireless network[15]. If a QoS Survey is impractical, this report can serve as a benchmark for how radio transmissions will behave in a factory environment.

4.4.4 Frequency Harmonization

Harmonization of the RF spectrum is an essential step in managing the performance and allocation of the spectral resources within the factory. Depending on the size and nature of the factory operation, management of the spectral resources can be critical to the availability of the wireless networks. The following are practical consideration in harmonization of the RF spectrum within a factory.

FCC Licensing – Obtaining a license from the United States Federal Communications Commission (FCC) to obtain the exclusive rights to a specific frequency in a well-defined geographic area.

Channelization – Assigning a specific channel within a frequency band to a specific device or wireless network, and allowing no other device to share that channel within the device's operating distance. This is applied where dependability and speed are paramount such as safety situations.

Multiplexing – Allowing multiple users to share a frequency using techniques such as time division, code division, phase shifting, and others. This is usually applied where there are many users and performance is less critical.

Proximity – Using low power devices at short distances between transmitter and receiver. This concept is applied where close proximity is practical and the impact of interference is minimal.

Pairing – Coupling a specific transmitter and specific receiver using identity codes.

Matching – Similar to pairing, but using groups of transmitters and groups of receivers so that any receiver in the group can work with any transmitter in the group.

Data Filtering – Applicable to handling the problem of "data flooding" when a passive Radio Frequency Identification (RFID) transceiver picks up tag data from different RFID usage domains. The filtering is sometimes included as a part of the RFID application software.

4.4.5 Topology and Node Placement

Some wireless networks allow for the selection of a topology. For example, ISA100.11a allows for the selection of mesh network and star topologies. Mesh and star both have strengths and weaknesses, for example in reliability and latency. To select the best topology for a wireless network, various aspects are considered such as the scalability, mobility, security, infrastructure, and the intended use of the wireless nodes. A brittle topology can create squeeze points in the network, placing a burden on one or more nodes, taxing battery life, and creating points of failure. The use of a certain topology can limit the number of nodes and the coverage of a wireless network. Hence, the expected growth of the wireless network determines the required number of access points and their coverage. Moreover, node mobility determines the need for roaming within the plant and the required speed for this roaming. Changes in the physical factory environment can occur, and where these changes can be anticipated, it is recommended to add routing or hand-off points such that service is not interrupted.

The processing needed for various security aspects determines the need of high processing nodes within each coverage area or that simple wireless nodes are enough to achieve the required security needs. Moreover, the existing infrastructure availability may make it easier to use a star topology, for example. Finally, amount of traffic generated or handled by a wireless node can also help in selecting a topology. As an example, field nodes with low data rates are commonly connected in a star topology to aggregate data before forwarding to the more congested parts of the network. Another example is back-haul nodes where point-to-point high data rate links are commonly used.

It is recommended that engineers consult vendor documentation. Vendors and service providers will often provide systems engineering guides that will help the designer to optimize the reliability of their network by providing best-practice guidance on node placement, the number of gateways, and device configuration (e.g., routing or non-routing).

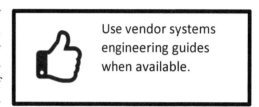

Use vendor systems engineering guides when available.

4.4.6 Simulation

Simulation is a good tool for reducing risk associated with complex designs or scenarios involving wireless supervisory or feedback control. Simulation allows for performance of the wireless system to be assessed before a major deployment investment is made. The accuracy of the simulation will rely on the fidelity of the model used. A high-fidelity model will produce more accurate results that match the real world; however, such accurate simulations require detailed knowledge of the radio environment and network behavior. Testing with actual equipment can be a more effective means of assessing performance; but simulation can be used to identify risk of the fully deployed system and is better suited for optimization than is trial-and-error network design. During network simulations, various networking performance metrics should be considered. These network aspects have been discussed in Section 4.3.1.2 where the system parameters are optimized to achieve the required performance levels. Furthermore, the node placement and network structure including the need of relays and their placement are investigated during these simulations.

For wireless systems involving feedback control or critical supervisory control, simulations are recommended to verify that a network design will meet the high-reliability requirements necessary for critical systems functions. Wireless networks are installed to achieve certain objectives in the industrial environment. To tune the design parameters and validate the ability of the wireless network to achieve

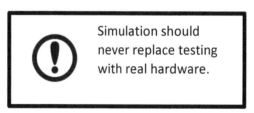

Simulation should never replace testing with real hardware.

these objectives, cyber-physical systems simulations should be used to predict performance. Simulations should include failure modes such as power loss to devices and infrastructure, RF interference, and changes in the physical environment that will lead to increased attenuation, signal loss, or exacerbated multi-path. Simulations that combine both a network and the physical model are often referred to as a co-simulation. Many tools exist for conducting simulations; however, co-simulations require effort to combine the physical simulator with the network simulator. When conducting a co-simulation, a model for the physical process is needed which can be generally simplified to virtually represent the process rate, inputs, and outputs. Moreover, the system dynamics and control algorithms are included to model the wireless network effects on the control loops. Furthermore, the interfaces between the physical system and the wireless network should be modeled including the difference in timing behaviors of both systems.

Simulation is a useful tool for verifying a network design or developing an optimal solution, but it should be used with caution and is better validated through testing. When wireless is used for control of an industrial system, testing should be an integral part of the design process.

4.5 Deployment and Monitoring

Once the system is designed, it must be deployed. Deployment involves installation, operation, and maintenance of the designed wireless network. Deployment can be divided into three major aspects which are the Deployment, Monitoring, and Updating. Deployment includes setup, testing, and training of the designed network. Setup entails installation of the networking equipment, configuration, and personnel training. Once installation is concluded, Monitoring and Analysis will commence. During this stage, the operational network will be monitored and will include spectrum sensing, capture of network statistics and traffic as necessary, cybersecurity event detection, and physical environment monitoring. Using data from monitoring and

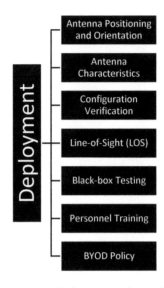

analysis, it is possible to make improvements to the network over time, extend the network, and tune the system such that performance is improved. Updating and Optimization is a process of continuous improvement. Continuous improvement will come from understanding the network and any considerations such as antenna position, frequency allocations, interference, and loading that may degrade network performance over time. Wireless networks operate very similar to wired networks with the main difference being the nature of the wireless medium through which communication is conducted.

4.5.1 Deployment

During Deployment, the wireless network hardware and software are installed and tested to achieve the designed performance levels. Proper antenna installation assures the delivery of wireless transmissions over the network. While technological capabilities of existing products may lead to specific technical requirements of the deployment, this section focuses on the general wireless networking aspects of deployment. Moreover, training on operating and managing the wireless network is essential at this stage to prevent any loss in performance due to human errors. The expected result of this phase is a fully operational wireless network which implements the intended design.

4.5.1.1 Antenna Positioning and Orientation

One major consideration in a wireless deployment is the placement of the antennas for each device. Antenna placement includes antenna positioning and orientation. In general, it is best to position the antennas of each device with clear visibility to the other devices to which it will connect. This can be achieved by placing antennas at high positions above machinery and other obstructions. One drawback to a higher antenna position is that it may increase the cable distance between the antenna and the wireless device. Increased cable distance will lead to increased transmit power loss and reduced receiver sensitivity. Installation according to manufacturer instructions and specifications will usually lead to optimal performance; however, it is important for the installer to be aware of the limitations on antenna cable extensions. Conversely, placing antennas close to the ground will introduce more power loss with distance and should be avoided. It is generally more advisable to incur cable losses to achieve appropriate antenna height than to position an antenna close to the ground.

Another aspect is antenna alignment which includes both the antenna polarization and radiation pattern. The antenna radiation pattern is a key consideration in optimal antenna placement. A traditional dipole "omni-directional" antenna is never truly omni-directional. In fact, these types of antennas radiate outward

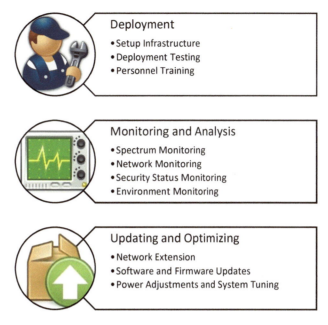

Figure 11. Steps to a Successful Wireless Deployment

with a toroidal pattern with a polarity that is parallel to the orientation of the antenna. Positioning such antennas high up on a ceiling will degrade performance of the wireless network. Common flat "pancake-style" Wi-Fi antennas are examples of sideways radiators. Although they appear to radiate downward, they radiate outward from the edges. Positioning such antennas high up will result in poor network performance unless the antenna pattern is designed to radiate downward and outward. Knowing the radiation pattern of any antenna is an important aspect in positioning an antenna.

4.5.1.2   Antenna Characteristics

As mentioned in the previous section, a crucial aspect during the deployment phase of the wireless network is the selection of antenna characteristics to match antenna placement and performance requirements. Considerations include antenna type, radiation pattern, and the number of antennas also called antenna diversity. The first major selection step is between omni-directional antennas and directional antennas. Omni-directional antennas are selected when the node can be connected to various nodes in various directions through the network operation. Conversely, directional antennas achieve better performance if the direction of the transmissions is fixed. Directional antennas can be electronically or mechanically steered. Electronic steering is not usually required for stationary deployments but is very useful for mobile applications. Omni-directional antennas are most useful for mesh style networks; whereas, directional antennas are more useful for microwave links and other long-haul connections. Directional antennas are also useful for device deployment on the perimeter of a factory. Assuming a well-designed model, the antenna will then be considered the most important contributor to establishing an effective link margin. Therefore, selecting an antenna with the appropriate characteristics for the position of the deployment is paramount for an effective operation.

4.5.1.3 Configuration Verification

Often the wireless network is deployed by a team different than those who designed the system. Therefore, a process for verifying that the network was deployed according to design intent is required. This would include visual inspection of installed devices and cables, as well as inspection of configuration and provisioning of the network equipment.

4.5.1.4 Establish Line-of-Sight (LOS) Links

The existence of an unobstructed LOS between wireless nodes improves the performance significantly. This is primarily a result of the LOS component of the transmission as seen by the receiver overpowering the other reflected components from objects in the factory. When a LOS component is missing, path loss between transmitter and receiver will increase

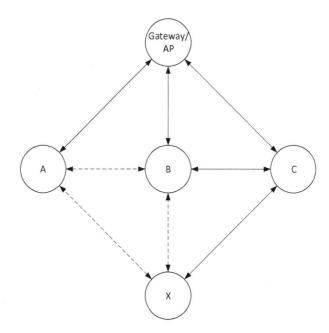

Figure 12. LOS links in a mesh network

significantly. The resulting multi-path reflection will distort the signal resulting in link reliability problems. As a result, it is highly recommended to establish a LOS communication link between each transmitter and receiver. For mesh networks, this is not usually possible or necessary; however, within a mesh network at least one LOS link should exist for each transmitter and at least one LOS route should exist between each transmitter and the centralized gateway devices if gateways exist. This is shown in Figure 12 where device X communicates with a complete LOS route to the gateway through its LOS counterpart, device C. It may be possible to communicate through nodes A and B effectively. One caveat to this general rule is that device C should have the resources (i.e., bandwidth, power, and processing speed) to accommodate the added load of the traffic from device X. It is important to follow the manufacturer's recommendations when establishing LOS connectivity and an effective network topology.

4.5.1.5 Black-box Test Methods

Factory operators, system integrators, and control systems designers are rarely experts in wireless communications systems. Considerations such as electromagnetic propagation, antenna efficiency, path loss exponents, packet error rates, and medium access are often foreign concepts to factory engineers. When available, link quality metrics such as packet loss ratios are informative but can be difficult to understand with complex mesh architectures and routing algorithms. The control system design will only need to know the statistical distribution of latency and reliability of information through the network to design a controller that is robust. Therefore, it is recommended that black-box tests be conducted for each installed device. Black-box tests are those types of tests that do not require internal performance metrics from the wireless device. Instead, black-box tests allow for performance evaluation using live process signals to measure reliability and latency. It is possible to construct black-box test harnesses; however, having network devices and infrastructure such as the PLC that support black-box tests makes evaluation much easier for the factory engineer.

4.5.1.6 Personnel Training on Network Operation

The operating personnel of the wireless network need to be trained on setup, administrating, and monitoring of the network. A certification process should be well defined to ensure the ability of personnel in performing the required networking tasks. The use of network diagnostic tools is another major task to deploy and maintain the network to be able to get the most out of the installed network.

4.5.1.7   Personnel Training on General Awareness of Wireless Networks

Wireless technology pervades everyday personal life. Employees operate cell phones and other personal electronic devices. These devices can interfere with the operation of the factory network as the employees may not be aware of the impacts of using their personal devices within the factory. To lessen the impact of personal devices on the factory network, it is recommended that employees are trained with a general knowledge of how wireless networks function and how personal devices can impact the performance of the factory network. For example, employees may bring cell phones with Wi-Fi hotspots turned on which can be disruptive. Another example could include proactive employees using personal walkie-talkies to be more productive or safe and disrupt the operation of a factory network in the process. Finally, educating employees about keeping microwave ovens clean can lessen EM leakage from the ovens and thereby lessen the impact to the factory wireless network.

4.5.1.8   Bring Your Own Device Policy

Another important aspect when designing a wireless solution is building or updating the bring your own device (BYOD) policy. This policy introduces the industrial environment regulations for using employees' own devices. The focus here is about wireless devices because of the interference and security issues that may be caused as a result of using these devices in the work environment.

Generally, certain work areas at which safety wireless signals are transmitted must have exclusive bands usage for the safety applications that may lead, in some scenarios, to restrict the usage of personal devices totally. A certain private wireless network may restrict device connection establishment to work non-personal devices. Moreover, certain types of wireless may be prohibited either due to their power level or continuous data transmission that may cause unacceptable interference.

4.5.2   Monitoring and Analysis

The operational wireless network is continually monitored to keep track of various parameters related to the network performance. Network monitoring includes continual monitoring of the EM spectrum, the performance of the network, the security state of the network and physical factory process, and the physical environment that impacts EM propagation.

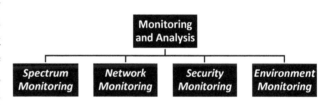

4.5.2.1   Spectrum Monitoring

Spectrum monitoring is performed in various stages while building a wireless network. It is performed initially within the site survey and later through the design stage where spectrum monitoring is performed while testing the designed network. During network operation, continual spectrum monitoring is recommended. A robust spectrum monitoring solution will include spectrum analytics, ability to correlate the spectral activity to factory activities, trends and prediction of spectrum usage, spectrum anomaly detection, geolocation of interference, and reporting. A spectrum monitoring solution will provide a complete situational awareness picture of the RF bands used by the factory operation and the interference patterns that could impact factory operation. In fact, it is possible that the spectrum monitoring solution be integrated with factory automation features such as PLCs.

4.5.2.2 Network Monitoring

Network monitoring is important as it includes various nodes' status, traffic patterns, routes, and statistics, link health and errors, and network topology. A network monitoring solution is usually used to monitor and analyze various network aspects. First, various nodes of the network are monitored to ensure that each one is active and correctly connected to intended nodes in the network. Backup nodes also may be checked to confirm availability for operating if needed. Various nodes are checked periodically through test messages and data exchange between nodes. Network monitoring will support factory engineers in assessing the location of bottlenecks, sources of data surges, hop patterns, and other considerations. It will also help engineers to assess if wireless devices need to be replaced, repaired, or adjusted, especially if a change in the environment has degraded performance. Many network monitoring tools exist in both open source and commercially. It is recommended that the product used is selected based on customization requirements and in-house knowledge of networking in general.

4.5.2.3 Security Monitoring

To monitor the network security status, statistics about the packet errors, failures, timeouts, and successes are evaluated. Like spectrum monitoring and network monitoring, security monitoring is a consideration that can be addressed through third-party products and solutions. Security monitoring will allow for the detection of abnormal network events such as unauthorized access, rogue devices, and suspicious network behavior that deviates from expected behavior. Security monitoring tools will provide deep-packet inspection and traffic pattern anomaly detection. The security monitoring feature may come as an option or feature of a network monitor or wireless product, or it might be a standalone feature such as wireless sniffers. The list of security products in both the open source and commercial domain is vast. A security monitoring product should be easy to use, support the protocols used within the factory, and integrate well within existing factory networks and reporting tools. For wireless networks, security monitoring could be built into the wireless devices or exist independent of the industrial operation. Wireless traffic sniffers exist and must be configured with the authentication materials of the operational network to be useful.

4.5.2.4 Environment Monitoring

The surroundings of wireless nodes will have a large impact on their performance. Therefore, stacking or moving of materials through the wireless links must be monitored. Metal as an example is highly reflective and can change wireless link behavior. Different materials may have different effects on the performance and hence monitoring is required to avoid scenarios where the planned wireless links change greatly because of the surrounding environment. Any intended change in the environment or configuration of the factory should undergo normal factory change management procedures. Change management procedures should include the possible performance impact to wireless networks.

4.5.3 Updates and Optimization

In an operational system, various network settings may need to be adjusted over time. Software and firmware may need to be updated, or the network may need to be extended. Continuous maintenance and optimization includes accommodating network extensions, performing software and firmware updates, and making antenna and power adjustments to wireless devices.

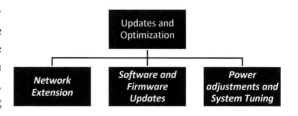

4.5.3.1 Network Extension

One of the major advantages of using wireless networks is the scalability of the network where new nodes can be added to the network conveniently. Often in an industrial network, the infrastructural components to the network are installed first and the devices themselves are later deployed. This is a common deployment style for industrial wireless mesh networks such as ISA100 Wireless and WirelessHART. By installing the infrastructure components first in such network types, the aggregator nodes can be placed to maximum coverage over the facility. Devices can then be added to the network as needed by the instrumentation, automation components, and data collection facilities.

In industrial mesh networks, the number of nodes allowed to connect to an access point is limited. When adding more nodes to a network, wireless resource allocation should be reviewed and revised accordingly to accommodate additional traffic. Testing of the network performance after extension is then required to verify the correct operation. However, adding a new node while the network is in operation must be done without a negative impact to the operational network. In a well-planned network, maximum throughput and network size are designed to accommodate new devices. In a time-division multiple access (TDMA) mesh network, gateway placement, topology, and scheduling are all designed with growth in mind. Therefore, when extending the network with new nodes, the device will only need to be physically installed with appropriate antenna placement, provisioned, and then powered on.

Whenever possible, simulation is a tool that can be used to validate a new design that will be added to the deployed system. Especially for feedback and supervisory control systems using wireless communication, simulation could be an essential step in avoiding a potential problem. It is high recommended to use simulation for wirelessly controlled system before any deployment.

When extending the network, all aspects of the wireless lifecycle can be repeated at a smaller scale including testing for performance, assessing the increased interference, and monitoring for traffic patterns and network topology. Afterwards, network parameter tuning and optimization can be performed on the new devices and the overall network to accommodate the new devices.

4.5.3.2   Software and Firmware Updates
Various network devices need firmware updates to fix discovered bugs, patch security holes, make performance enhancements, and add new features. Periodic checking for the availability of the updates is recommended; however, automatic installation of updates is not recommended. Before applying any update to software or firmware, the update must be validated through testing first before rolling out to the deployed network. Steps involved with rolling out updates to software and firmware include the following:

- Extensive testing of the update within a controlled environment
- Configuration management of the existing system with roll-back capability
- Deployment plan developed and approved according to internal governance policies
- Authorization of the update through internal governance policies

An operational factory system is very different from a typical non-operational office system. Application of software or firmware updates to the wireless network or any component with in the factory operation could result in downtime. It is highly recommended that all updates are thoroughly researched and tested before deployment.

4.5.3.3   Power Adjustments and Reporting Rate Tuning
Tuning the transmission power of wireless nodes allows for less interference and more control of nodes associating with other network nodes. Increased transmit power is not necessarily an improvement. Increasing transmit power can lead to better performance for one device on a network, but it can also lead to shorter battery life. Increased transmit power may also lower performance of other devices on adjacent wireless networks using the same RF band. A different approach to tuning transmit power is to develop a link budget and maintaining a defined link margin to accommodate unexpected interference or a change in the environment. Developing a link budget for each device is a common method for accomplishing this task; however, many wireless systems will employ automatic power control which adjusts transmit power

to reach quality of service thresholds but without disadvantaging other devices or shortening battery life. Power adjustments account for regulations that limit the radiated power from an antenna.

Report rate tuning is the process for setting the transmission rate for a given device. The reporting rate will determine how often process variables that are monitored by a network device are transmitted. A high reporting will result in more transmissions and more bandwidth and battery utilization. If the rate is set to be too high, other wireless device transmissions may fail, and, if the reporting rate is set to be too low, the assigned bandwidth will be wasted. Reporting rates should be set according to the process design requirements. Later adjustments should be made in accordance with new process requirements or network reliability requirements which are usually derived from process requirements. Rate adaptation is usually accomplished through manual intervention; however, automatic reporting rates can be applied to adjust to conditions within the factory and the wireless network.

5   WIRELESS FOR SAFETY

Wireless systems may be useful to enhancing the safety profile within a factory operation. These systems can be used to prevent injury through improved communication and enhanced situational awareness within the factory. Wireless safety systems are used in many applications including those designed to prevent chemical handling mishaps, avoid heavy equipment accidents such as "struck-by, and back-over" incidents, prevent falls through active position monitoring and safety interconnects, provide situational awareness within confined spaces, and improve safety for non-employees.

Along with adaption of wireless sensor networks for industrial automation, there are more applications of wireless technology created by users after they are more familiar and comfortable with the wireless technology. Also because of the strong benefits of wireless applications that can save project execution time and cost, more and more wireless has been used for secondary or backup systems for time-critical application such as safety or control applications. Based on this movement, ISA-84 working group (WG) 8 developed a technical report on wireless for safety systems other than those of a safety integrated system (SIS), i.e., those systems with a system integrity level (SIL) rating below ten. The technical report describes the additional elements needed to be addressed when wireless technology is used in an Independent Protection Layer (IPL). Refer to the ISA technical report TR84.00.08-2017 *Guidance for Application of Wireless Sensor Technology to Non-SIS Independent Protection Layers* for more information[13].

6   INDUSTRIAL WIRELESS SECURITY

Industrial control systems (ICS) cybersecurity is a branch of general cybersecurity in which the systems being protected have physical characteristics which if compromised can lead to down-time, injury or death, and economic loss. Industrial control systems include supervisory control and data acquisition (SCADA) systems, localized work-cells, enterprise control systems, and cloud-based factory collection systems. Traditional information technology (IT) systems differ from operational technology (OT) systems primarily in their cybersecurity priorities. In general, IT systems defend against data extractions. Encryption used to provide confidentiality is of primary concern. In OT systems, confidentiality is no longer of paramount concern. While eavesdropping can lead to reverse engineering of proprietary factory methods and design, it is usually more important to keep the factory running. Therefore, technologies must assure that both cybersecurity controls and cyber-attack do not limit or prevent the capability of the factory running with high availability. Table 7 lists the priorities of IT and OT systems. It is important for IT professionals to recognize that wireless security practices used in the office may not be available for factory deployments. If they are available, they may not be desirable to maintain system availability. Securing the industrial network can be summarized in the following considerations: Secure the physical environment; Secure the end-points; Secure the controller; and Secure network transmissions/data. Industrial wireless networks have the same consideration as wired networks with the addition of protecting the electromagnetic spectrum allocated for the industrial wireless network operation.

Table 7. Typical Priorities of IT and OT Systems

Priority	IT	OT
Highest	Confidentiality	Availability
...	Integrity	Authenticity
...	Authenticity	Integrity
Lowest	Availability	Confidentiality

The number of devices connecting to industrial networks is increasing at a rapid rate. It exposes systems to security breaches and cyberattacks. As a result, security is paramount for industrial operations. Some manufacturers think wireless will create new vulnerabilities in the network that may result in potential threats. Just making the wireless network accessible through a password is not adequate. One key concern is how to identity and eliminate rogue access points. Therefore, wireless intrusion detection systems and intrusion prevention systems are in demand.

In addition, isolation of production devices on a separate network from corporate networks, internet traffic, and phone and surveillance systems is necessary. In other words, one can employ an "island" approach to networking that limits the movement of traffic and devices between islands. By properly segmenting a network, it can limit movement between networks to appropriate devices and block the movement of devices that are unnecessary or provide little value.

6.1 Practical Considerations

Plant operators should follow manufacturer guidance for security where it does not conflict with recognized guidance and best-practices.

Ease of Implementation – Make securing wireless deployments easy to implement and maintain

Physical security – Physically protect wireless access points, gateways, modems, and devices

Default security – Auto-configure network devices to the highest security level by default

Updates – Securely update software, firmware, and data over-the-air or wire and disable automatic updates

Share and Report – Share security threat data, perform analytics, and continually learn about security

Trust – Form a network of digital trust and protect data and privacy as practical and possible.

Full life-cycle – Securely operate the network across the entire lifecycle from product development through deployment

Passwords – Do not use default passwords once the system is installed; protect passwords; authenticate users; enforce password change policies

Zones and Conduits – Separate industrial networks into zones and conduits and separate the industrial network from the enterprise office network; apply policies to industrial networks separate from the enterprise network (refer to IEC 62443[3])

Spectrum Monitoring – Use spectrum monitoring to gain awareness of normal versus abnormal wireless activity

Network Monitoring – Monitor the industrial network continually and non-intrusively without compromising factory operations

6.2   Security Assessments, Reporting, and Training

The Industrial Control Systems Cyber Emergency Response Team (ICS-CERT) was established to maintain a database of security incidents, share mitigation methods, and provide training and tools for assessing risk within an ICS. If a security incident does occur, it is recommended that the incident be reported to ICS-CERT. The ICS-CERT home page may be found at https://ics-cert.us-cert.gov/.

6.3   Normative Security References

For more information on how to implement a security program within an industrial enterprise, the following guidelines and standards are available.

[16] K. Stouffer, T. Zimmerman, C. Tang, J. Lubell, J. Cichonski, and J. McCarthy, "Cybersecurity framework manufacturing profile," Gaithersburg, MD, Sep. 2017.

[17] K. Stouffer, V. Pillitteri, S. Lightman, M. Abrams, and A. Hahn, "Guide to Industrial Control Systems (ICS) Security," Gaithersburg, MD, Jun. 2015.

[18] "Security and Privacy Controls for Federal Information Systems and Organizations," Gaithersburg, MD, Apr. 2013.

[19] M. P. Souppaya and K. A. Scarfone, "Guidelines for securing Wireless Local Area Networks (WLANs)," Gaithersburg, MD, 2012.

[3] (International Electrotechnical Commission), "ISO/IEC-62443 Security for industrial automation and control systems," 2018.

7 BEST PRACTICE CONSIDERATIONS

7.1 Antenna Placement and the Fresnel Distance

When setting up antennas, if possible be certain to maintain a direct line-of-sight (LOS) path between each transmitter and receiver that are intended to communicate together. Even in a mesh network in which multi-hop communications is intended, each hop should be designed to have LOS. Some devices are designed to accommodate non-line-of-sight (NLOS) communications; however, LOS is preferable to maximize reliability and reduce delay from retransmissions. In addition, obstructions such as those shown in the tank farm in Figure 13 should be kept well out of the LOS path to avoid diffractive effects. A good rule of thumb to optimize performance in this case is to calculate the first Fresnel zone distance, F_1, and assure that objects do not come within that radius from the mid-point of the LOS path. The first Fresnel zone is calculated as $F_1 = \sqrt{\lambda d_1 d_2 / (d_1 + d_2)}$ where the wavelength $\lambda = c / f$. Distances are in meters. The constant, c, is the speed of light, which is 3×10^8 meters per second, and f is the transmit frequency in Hz. In an indoor facility, obtaining the clearance is not always possible and will not usually become a root cause of serious link degradation. It should also be noted that the Fresnel zone equation is a function of distance and wavelength. Lower frequency bands will convert to larger wavelengths and, therefore, have larger Fresnel clearances. This has implications for densely populated indoor facilities in that lower frequency RF deployments will not always perform better than higher-frequency deployments due to Fresnel clearance as it would in a less dense outdoor installation. Testing of devices before final deployment will confirm that performance requirements will be met.

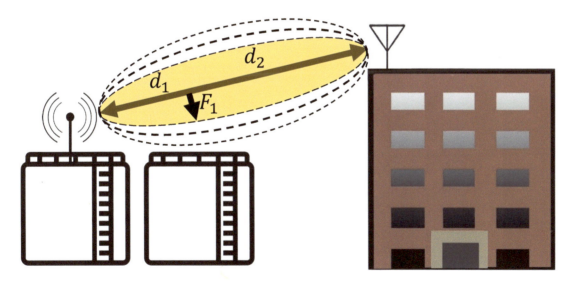

Figure 13. Antenna Height using the Fresnel Distance

39

7.2 Obstructions and Path Redundancy

Shadowing occurs when an object causes an electromagnetic blockage like a shadow caused by visible light. Both visible light and RF waves are forms of electromagnetic radiation in the form of waves or photons. An RF shadow is therefore a deep attenuation of the electromagnetic energy in a specific region caused when RF waves are blocked. For example, when a large object, such as a commercial jetliner, rolls into an area and sufficiently blocks the direct path between transmitter and receiver, the link between the two may be lost. In many circumstances, diffraction and multipath will serve to overcome a blockage of the direct path with an increase in data loss or delay. Often the transmitted signal is attenuated beyond signal recovery and another solution is required to maintain quality of service requirements.

The solution depends entirely on the wireless network being deployed and the minimum requirements for the applications using the wireless network. One option includes transmitting from a different location. This is often possible using lightweight access points in IEEE 802.11 and 802.15.4 networks; however, hand-off from one access point to the other can be too slow. Other options include a multi-hop solution as shown in Figure 14. Using a multi-hop solution could require anticipating the blockage and planning for an alternate fixed communication path or redundant path. Another solution would use a more active form of a mesh network in which nodes within the network maintain constant awareness of link quality and act accordingly. An IEEE 802.11 network that uses OSI layer 2 metrics can respond faster to changes in the environment than one that uses layer 3 metrics; however every networking technology has different capabilities. The key concept here is the use of transmission path redundancy to improve the resilience of the network to changes in the environment. Use path redundancy to improve network reliability within an environment where the RF characteristics can change. Most industrial environments fall into this category to some degree. Many wireless systems support path diversity, and including ISA100 Wireless, WirelessHART, Wi-Fi, ZigBee, and proprietary solutions.

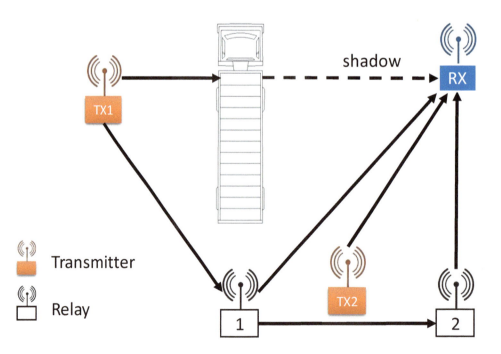

Figure 14. Overcoming Shadowing

7.3 Difficult-To-Reach Locations

Narrow corridors, tight spaces, areas occluded with machines, and applications low to the ground make wireless connectivity difficult. Many industrial applications require connectivity with hard to reach areas. Running cables is often not an option making wireless the only option. Examples include rows of machines with overhead gantry systems in an automobile assembly factory as shown in Figure 15. In this scenario, two rows of machines create a canyon effect. If a wireless device is stationed within the canyon, connectivity to the device would be unreliable. One option would be to raise the antenna height of the wireless device such that a LOS connection is possible; however, not all devices or antennas can be moved or relocated. Another possible solution makes use of the multipath environment. Machines are often enclosed in highly reflective metal boxes. Since RF signals reflect well off most flat metal surfaces, antennas could be positioned to make use of the reflected energy.

In the figure, Antenna 1 uses the reflected energy off the adjacent machine to maintain connection with the access point mounted on the wall. Antenna 2, must be positioned higher since the adjacent wall is made of concrete which is not a good RF reflector. If the wall happened to be made of sheet metal, then it would be possible to use multi-path in the same way as Antenna 1. An important consideration is how often the layout of the factory changes. Frequent changes in the location of machines could make such an installation more prone to quality of service fluctuations.

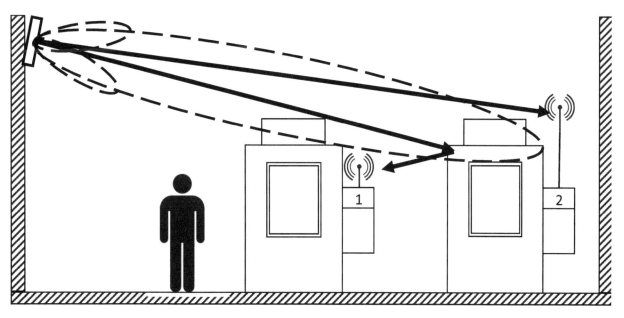

Figure 15. Overcoming Metal Canyons

7.4 Non-Production Emitters such as Microwave Ovens

Many common devices such as microwave ovens, cell phone hotspots, automobile hotspots, video games, baby monitors, personal Bluetooth devices, and others will emit RF energy. These devices can interfere with factory wireless operations, and steps should be taken to mitigate impacts through technological, educational, and policy enforcement. The microwave oven is discussed in this section. Microwave ovens are an important source of RF interference. Because these devices generate electromagnetic waves within the 2400 MHz ISM band where many industrial wireless networks operate, they can severely degrade the performance of the networks by introducing RF interference. The amount of interference will depend on the proximity of the ovens to the network devices. Industrial networks will often experience network failures during scheduled lunch breaks when one or more microwave ovens are used for extended periods of time. To reduce or eliminate the impacts of microwave ovens on an industrial wireless network, the following steps should be followed. Some of these steps are illustrated in Figure 16.

Distance - Keep microwave ovens in a room far away from the industrial operation. The intensity of the microwave oven interference will decrease with distance.

Oven Quality – Chose microwave ovens that are high quality and well shielded. A commercial rating does not indicate quality or shielding capability. Testing microwave ovens for interference levels at progressively increasing distance using a spectrum analyzer may be of benefit.

Containing Room – Place the ovens in a designated room such as a lunch room or adjacent room with a metal door. If the room is near to the factory operation, it may be necessary to shield the room. Metal foil can be applied to walls, doors, and windows to contain the interference but can be a costly investment. Windows can be covered or shielded to prevent interference leakage.

Change RF Band – Move the factory wireless network to another band such as 900 MHz band or 5 GHz. Microwave ovens impact the upper half of the 2.4 GHz ISM band more than the lower half[20]; therefore, it may be possible to limit the operation of the industrial wireless network to channels at the lower end of the 2.4 GHz band, for example, channels below 2.44 GHz.

Cleaning – Keeping microwave ovens clean can prevent EM leakage.

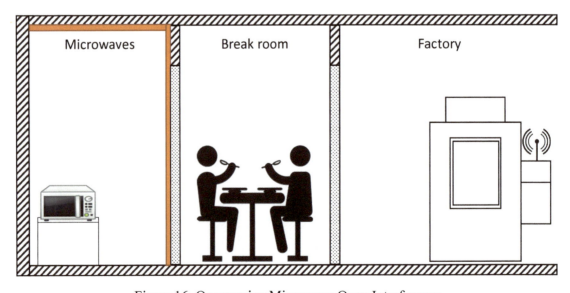

Figure 16. Overcoming Microwave Oven Interference

7.5 Confined Space Gas Sensing and Safety Applications

Confined spaces are present in many plants and factories. Tanks, large pipes, manholes, boilers, and painting rooms are examples of confined spaces. Various communications scenarios may occur at confined spaces including environment monitoring, voice communications, and human occupancy identifications. Most of these are safety-related applications and hence reliable communications are required.

One of the major safety applications in confined spaces is gas sensing and air quality monitoring. Generally, confined spaces present a threat to safety from the accumulation of poisonous or combustible gases such as oxygen, carbon monoxide, benzene, and hydrogen sulfide. Confined spaces have poor ventilation leading to gas accumulation. It is also difficult to evacuate personnel when a dangerous situation does occur. Wireless gas sensors are used for the detection of gases prior to entering a confined space and for continuous monitoring to maintain continuous safety. While wireless sensors are a useful technology to help maintain a safe working environment, it is important to understand the challenges of wireless when used in confined spaces. Figure 17 shows an illustration of a gas sensing in confined spaces. In this scenario, a man is welding in a confined space. The welding torch is producing carbon monoxide gas. The entry to the space is small with an adjacent manhole and ladder. Evacuation from the space would be difficult if ventilation fails and poisonous gases accumulate. In this and similar scenarios, the following actions would help to maintain safety using a wireless sensor network.

RF Environment – Understand the materials of the confined space and how radio waves propagate within it. Spaces with metal walls will reflect radio waves whereas concrete will absorb the RF waves.

Testing – Understand latency and reliability of each wireless solution with thorough testing before using a wireless gas sensing application in a live scenario. Sensor applications should support black-box testing.

Antenna Placement – Place sensors and relay nodes to maximize LOS communication. Align antennas to maximize receive power and polarization alignment.

Redundancy – Use multiple sensors within the confined space in case one fails.

Intrinsic Safety – Select wireless devices that meet applicable intrinsic safety standards.

Common Sense – Do not allow technology to override or replace common sense practices.

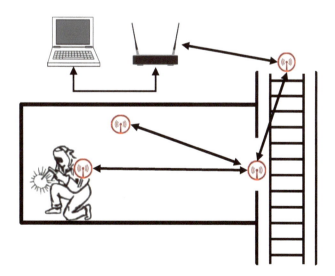

Figure 17. Wireless Sensors in Confined Spaces

Within the aerospace industry some mechanics work in difficult conditions inside commercial aircraft confined spaces such as fuel tanks and wing structure. To protect their safety, a two-way radio is assigned to each employee and checked out through a registration process. A responsible attendant monitors all the entrants at a command center by periodically sending communication signals and text messages to them. A typical work effort in confined space involves handling sealants and chemicals thereby requiring constant surveillance. Gas detectors may use multiple sensors looking for oxygen level and presence of hazardous gases such as carbon monoxide. Other requirements may include lower explosive level detectors, and photo ionization sensors engineered to detect volatile organic compounds. The safety devices continuously monitor the air quality and transmit text and voice data. In addition, Bluetooth beacons communicate with entrant radios to report the location of the workers within the factory. In emergency situations such as building evacuation, the wireless safety system will inform the employees to leave their work areas.

8 REFERENCES

[1]   R. Candell, "Industrial wireless systems workshop proceedings," Gaithersburg, MD, May 2017.

[2]   K. Stouffer, V. Pillitteri, S. Lightman, M. Abrams, and A. Hahn, "Guide to Industrial Control Systems (ICS) Security," Gaithersburg, MD, Jun. 2015.

[3]   (International Electrotechnical Commission), "ISO/IEC-62443 Security for industrial automation and control systems," 2018.

[4]   IEEE, "IEEE 802.11," *IEEE Std 802.11-2012 (Revision of IEEE Std 802.11-2007)*, vol. 2012, no. March. p. 2793, 2012.

[5]   IEEE 802.15.4, *IEEE standard for Information Technology 802.15.4, Wireless Medium Access Control (MAC) and Physical layer (PHY) specifications for low-rate wireless personal area networks (LR-WPANs)*, vol. 2006, no. September. 2006.

[6]   V. C. Gungor and G. P. Hancke, "Industrial Wireless Sensor Networks: Challenges, Design Principles, and Technical Approaches," *Ind. Electron. IEEE Trans.*, vol. 56, no. 10, pp. 4258–4265, 2009.

[7]   M. Luvisotto, Z. Pang, and D. Dzung, "Ultra High Performance Wireless Control for Critical Applications: Challenges and Directions," *IEEE Trans. Ind. Informatics*, vol. 13, no. 3, pp. 1448–1459, Jun. 2017.

[8]   "FCC OET Bulletin 65, Biological Effects and Potential Hazards of Radio frequency Electromagnetic Fields," Washington, 1999.

[9]   A. S. Tanenbaum and D. J. Wetherall, *Computer Networks 5th By Andrew S. Tanenbaum (International Economy Edition)*. Prentice Hall, Indian International Ed., 2010.

[10]   (National Fire National Fire Protection Association), *National Electrical Code NFPA Std. 70*. 2017.

[11]   Z. Pang, M. Luvisotto, and D. Dzung, "Wireless High-Performance Communications: The Challenges and Opportunities of a New Target," *IEEE Ind. Electron. Mag.*, vol. 11, no. 3, pp. 20–25, Sep. 2017.

[12]   (National Telecommunications and Information Administration), "NTIA Frequency Allocation Chart." [Online]. Available: https://www.ntia.doc.gov/page/2011/united-states-frequency-allocation-chart.

[13]   (International Society of Automation), "ISA-TR84.00.08-2017, Guidance for Application of Wireless Sensor Technology to Non-SIS Independent Protection Layers," 2017.

[14]   R. Candell *et al.*, "Industrial wireless systems radio propagation measurements," Gaithersburg, MD, Jan. 2017.

[15]   M. Damsaz, D. Guo, J. Peil, W. Stark, N. Moayeri, and R. Candell, "Channel modeling and performance of Zigbee radios in an industrial environment," in *2017 IEEE 13th International Workshop on Factory Communication Systems (WFCS)*, 2017, pp. 1–10.

[16]   K. Stouffer, T. Zimmerman, C. Tang, J. Lubell, J. Cichonski, and J. McCarthy, "Cybersecurity framework manufacturing profile," Gaithersburg, MD, Sep. 2017.

[17]   K. Stouffer, V. Pillitteri, S. Lightman, M. Abrams, and A. Hahn, "Guide to Industrial Control Systems

(ICS) Security," Gaithersburg, MD, Jun. 2015.

[18]   "Security and Privacy Controls for Federal Information Systems and Organizations," Gaithersburg, MD, Apr. 2013.

[19]   M. P. Souppaya and K. A. Scarfone, "Guidelines for securing Wireless Local Area Networks (WLANs)," Gaithersburg, MD, 2012.

[20]   P. Iturri *et al.*, "Impact of High Power Interference Sources in Planning and Deployment of Wireless Sensor Networks and Devices in the 2.4 GHz Frequency Band in Heterogeneous Environments," *Sensors*, vol. 12, no. 12, pp. 15689–15708, Nov. 2012.

Appendix A   Checklists

A-1. Defining Objectives Checklist

Checklist Item	Status
Project kick-off and stakeholders defined	
Clearly enumerate and define objectives	
Define how wireless will support objectives	
Define how wireless performance will be measured and how wireless performance directly correlates to enterprise objectives.	
Define how wireless in general will grow over time within the factory enterprise.	
Develop a security management plan for the operation.	
Conduct a preliminary spectral occupancy survey within the factory.	
Establish or update the spectrum management plan.	

A-2. Factory Survey Checklist

Checklist Item	Status
Review the role that wireless technology will take in meeting enterprise objectives.	
Review how wireless performance will be measured and how wireless performance directly correlates to enterprise objectives.	
Review the security risk level.	
Update the security plan for the operation.	
Conduct a thorough spectral occupancy survey • *Identify existing wireless devices and operating bands* • *Identify sources of EMI*	
Update the spectrum management plan.	
Update security management plan.	
Assess the existing physical factory design. Obtain factory inventory to include the following: Physical layout, operational model, measurement points, control points, machines, materials, monitoring systems, and databases	
Select points in which wireless will be used to monitor or control the operation	
Identify mobile devices and uses	
Determine signal specifications	
Determine technical requirements to meet the performance constraints of downstream data analysis, monitoring, and control applications. • *Number of Devices* • *Latency* • *Reliability* • *Throughput* • *Sensitivity analysis* • *Future growth potential*	
Identify power sources that may be leveraged	
Identify safety issues	

A-3. Candidate Selection Checklist

Checklist Item	Status
Review the role wireless technology will take in meeting enterprise objectives.	
Review how wireless performance will be measured and how wireless performance directly correlates to enterprise objectives.	
Review the security management plan and objectives.	
Develop a security plan for the operation.	
Conduct a thorough spectral occupancy survey • *Identify existing wireless devices* • *Identify existing operating bands* • *Identify sources of EMI*	
Update the spectrum management plan.	
Update security management plan.	
Assess the existing physical factory design. Obtain factory inventory to include the following: physical layout, operational model, measurement points, control points, machines, materials, monitoring systems, and databases	
Select points in which wireless will be used to monitor or control the operation	
Identify mobile devices and uses.	
Determine signal specifications.	
Determine technical requirements to meet the performance constraints of downstream data analysis, monitoring, and control applications. • *Number of Devices* • *Latency* • *Reliability* • *Throughput* • *Sensitivity analysis* • *Future growth potential*	
Identify power sources that may be leveraged.	
Identify safety issues.	
Identify needs of regulatory approval to operate for each candidate	
Define cost targets	
Define past-performance evaluation criteria and compare to the candidates	
Assess requirements compliance for each candidate.	

A-4. Candidate Scoring Checklist

Requirement	Weight	Specification	Candidate 1	Candidate 2	...	Candidate N
RF Operating Band	1	902 to 928 MHz	1	1		1
Range	1	30 meters	1	1		1
Latency	1	100 milliseconds	1	0		1
Data Delivery Reliability	1	99%	1	1		1
Reboot to Operation Time	1	< 30 seconds	1	1		0
Over-the-air re-keying	0.75	Yes/No	0	1		0
Number of Devices	0.8	100	1	1		1
Power source	0.6	24 VDC	1	1		1
Battery Life	1	1 year	1	1		1
Interoperation	1	OPC-UA	1	1		1
Maintainability	0.75	Qualitative	0.8	0.9		0.5
Security Compliant	1	Yes/No	1	1		1
Regulatory Compliant	1	Yes/No	1	1		1
Intrinsic safety rating	1	Class 1, Div. 2	1	1		1
Training Provided	0.5	Yes/No	1	1		1
Simplicity of Use	0.5	Qualitative	1	1		1
Price	0.75	Under $X	1	1		1
Past performance	0.75	Two written	1	0.5		0
Weight Sum (Score)			13.5	12.95		11.525

A-5. Wireless Design Checklist

Checklist Item	Status
Review objectives with stakeholders	
Review technical requirements	
Radio frequency characterization • *Direct measurement through site survey* • *Indirectly through link budget analysis*	
Frequency allocation plan	
Design network architecture	
Interoperability interfaces and protocols	
Perform factory software modifications • *Database Upgrades* • *Interface Upgrades* • *Logic Upgrades (PLC/Software/Firmware)* • *Analysis Reporting tools and integration*	
Develop spectrum monitoring plan	
Interference mitigation plan	
Develop security plan	
Performance measurement plan, preliminary	
Develop deployment plan for the selected candidates	
Develop a training plan	
Develop or update BYOD Policies	
Develop a roll-out plan for the wireless deployment	

A-6. Wireless Deployment Checklist

Checklist Item	Status
Review objectives with stakeholders	
Review technical requirements	
Review design and roll-out plan	
Roll-out network (iteratively)	
Verification of deployment to design	
Perform continuous training	
Performance wireless awareness training	
Implement spectrum monitoring plan	
Implement security management plan	
Implement wireless performance monitoring	
Validate that deployment meets design intention	
Schedule and perform regular maintenance	

Appendix B   Wireless Applicability Matrix

Table 8. Wireless applicability matrix for industrial processes

		Flow-based					Job-based						Safety				Back-haul				Tracking					Security						Remote			Maint.		
		Process Monitoring	Supervisory Control	Feedback Control	Alarm Conditions	In-situ Inspection	Factory Monitoring	Assembly: Sensing	Assembly: Actuation	Robots: Supervision	Robots: Feedback Control	Quality Inspection	Fall Prevention	Confined Spaces	Critical Event Detection	Human-Machine Colocation	Nearby or Indoor	Distant: LOS	Distant: BLOS	Geographically Remote	Indoor Machine Localization	Materials in Storage	Materials in Production	Tools	Personnel	Voice and Video Communication	Video Surveillance	Drone-based Surveillance	Grounds Control	Spectrum Monitoring Data	Personnel Authorization	Well-head Monitoring	Pipeline Monitoring	Tank Level Monitoring	Machine Health Monitoring	Building Automation	Augmented Reality
Home/Office	802.11	●	●	◐	◐	-	●	◐	◐	◐	◐	◐	◐	○	◐	◐	●	●	●	-	☆	⌁	⌁	⌁	⌁	●	●	●	◐	●	●	◐	◐	◐	◐	◐	●
	802.15.1	◐	○	◐	○	-	○	◐	◐	◐	◐	●	◐	◐	◐	◐	○	○	○	○	○	○	⌁	●	⌁	▶	▶	▶	○	○	◐	○	○	○	◐	○	▶
Industrial	802.15.4 TDMA	●	●	◐	◐	-	●	◐	◐	◐	◐	◐	◐	◐	◐	○	▶	▶	▶	▶	◐	⌁	⌁	⌁	◐	▶	▶	▶	◐	▶	○	●	●	●	○	●	▶
	802.15.4 CSMA	◐	◐	○	◐	-	◐	◐	◐	◐	◐	◐	◐	◐	◐	○	▶	▶	▶	▶	◐	⌁	⌁	⌁	◐	▶	▶	▶	◐	○	○	●	☆	◐	●	●	▶
	802.11 TDMA	☆	☆	☆	☆	-	☆	☆	☆	☆	☆	☆	☆	☆	☆	☆	-	-	▶	-	☆	⌁	⌁	⌁	-	▶	-	▶	☆	-	-	☆	☆	◐	☆	☆	-
	VLBR WAN	●	●	○	○	-	●	◐	◐	◐	◐	◐	◐	○	◐	○	▶	▶	▶	▶	◐	◐	◐	◐	◐	▶	◐	▶	◐	○	○	○	○	◐	◐	◐	○
Satellite	Geostationary	◐	◐	○	○	○	○	○	○	○	○	○	○	○	○	○	○	○	◐	◐	○	○	○	○	○	◐	◐	◐	○	○	◐	◐	◐	◐	◐	○	◐
	Low-earth Orbit	◐	◐	○	○	○	○	○	○	○	○	○	○	○	○	○	○	○	◐	◐	○	○	○	○	○	◐	◐	◐	○	○	◐	◐	◐	◐	◐	○	◐
	VLBR WAN	●	●	○	○	○	◐	○	○	○	○	◐	◐	○	○	○	▶	▶	▶	▶	○	○	○	○	◐	▶	◐	▶	☆	-	☆	○	○	○	◐	○	▶
Tracking	RFID	-	-	-	○	-	-	-	-	-	-	-	-	-	-	-	-	-	-	-	○	●	●	●	●	-	○	○	-	-	◐	-	○	-	○	-	-
Optical	Visible	○	○	○	○	○	☆	☆	☆	☆	☆	☆	☆	☆	☆	☆	○	○	○	○	☆	○	☆	☆	○	○	○	○	○	○	○	○	○	○	☆	○	○
	Infrared	○	○	○	○	○	☆	☆	☆	☆	☆	☆	☆	☆	☆	☆	○	○	○	○	☆	○	☆	☆	○	○	○	○	○	○	○	○	○	○	☆	☆	○
	Free-space	○	◐	○	◐	-	○	○	○	○	○	○	●	●	●	○	○	●	●	○	●	○	○	○	○	●	●	●	☆	●	●	●	●	●	○	◐	●
Cellular	Legacy	◐	○	○	○	-	○	◐	○	○	○	○	◐	◐	◐	◐	●	◐	◐	◐	○	○	○	○	○	◐	◐	◐	◐	◐	●	◐	◐	●	◐	▶	▶
	4G	◐	◐	○	○	-	◐	◐	○	○	○	○	◐	◐	◐	◐	◐	◐	◐	◐	○	○	○	○	○	◐	◐	◐	●	◐	●	◐	◐	◐	○	○	○
	5G	☆	☆	☆	☆	-	☆	☆	☆	☆	☆	☆	☆	☆	☆	☆	○	○	●	○	☆	☆	☆	☆	☆	☆	☆	☆	☆	☆	☆	☆	☆	☆	☆	☆	☆
Land-mobile	All types	○	○	-	○	-	○	○	○	○	○	○	○	◐	◐	◐	◐	◐	○	○	◐	◐	○	○	○	◐	●	●	●	◐	◐	○	○	○	○	◐	○
Specialty	Leaky Coax	◐	◐	-	◐	◐	◐	-	-	◐	◐	-	◐	◐	◐	-	◐	◐	○	○	◐	●	●	○	●	○	○	○	●	●	●	○	○	☆	○	◐	○

Legend: ● Fully supports problem domain, ◐ Partially supports problem domain but may have practicality, throughput, latency, reliability, or energy limitations, ⌁ Energy requirements limit applicability, ▶ Network throughput severely limits applicability, ◑ Network latency limits applicability, ○ Network latency precludes applicability, ☆ Future technology may support problem domain, ○ Not recommended, - Not considered